SCIENCE SORTED

Space, black holes and stuff

Glenn Murphy received his master's degree in science communication from London's Imperial College of Science, Technology and Medicine. He wrote his first popular science book, *Why Is Snot Green?*, while managing the Explainer team at the Science Museum in London. In 2007 he moved to the United States. He now lives and works in Raleigh, North Carolina, with his wife, Heather, and two unusually large and ill-tempered cats.

Favourite science fact: the eye of a colossal squid measures 27 cm (almost a foot) across. It has the largest eyes of any animal in the world.

Glenn is currently writing his ninth book.

SCIENCE SORTED

Space, black holes and stuff

By Glenn Murphy

Illustrated by Mike Phillips

MACMILLAN CHILDREN'S BOOKS

This book is produced in association with the Science Museum.
Royalties from the sale of this product help fund the
museum's exhibitions and programmes.

The Science Museum, London Internationally recognized as one
of the world's leading science centres. It contains more than 10,000
amazing exhibits, two fantastic simulator rides and the astounding
IMAX cinema. Enter a world of discovery and achievement, where
you can see, touch and experience real objects and icons
which have shaped the world we live in today or visit
www.sciencemuseum.org.uk to find out more.

First published 2010 by Macmillan Children's Books
a division of Macmillan Publishers Limited
20 New Wharf Road, London N1 9RR
Basingstoke and Oxford
Associated companies throughout the world
www.panmacmillan.com

ISBN 978-0-330-50893-3

1 3 5 7 9 8 6 4 2

A CIP catalogue record for this book is available from
the British Library.

Printed and bound in the UK by CPI Mackays, Chatham ME5 8TD

To Heather – still my favourite person to see stars with

Thanks to:

Gaby Morgan – for her patience, perseverance and tireless efforts in editing.

Jude Weston – for his scientific expertise, and for patiently explaining the concept of mass to his mum.

Deborah Bloxam, Ali Boyle, Doug Millard, Tom Vine, Deborah Jones and everyone else at the Science Museum who continue to offer their support and expertise.

The students and teachers of the Carolina Friends School, NC – your incredible enthusiasm for science inspired me, just when I needed it most.

Scot and Diane Schwichow – stars in their own right.

Russ Campbell and Roger Harris – keeping the dream of pub-based science communication alive.

Tracey Ridgewell for all her work designing the book.

And, as always, the Murphs and the Witts – without your support (and stealthy word-of-mouth marketing efforts) I would of course be quite lost.

Contents

1.
Hang on a Minute – What Is the Universe?

That is a very, very good question. One that most people don't bother to ask.

But then you're cleverer than most people, aren't you? After all, you're reading this book. I bet you're always asking tricky and interesting questions like that. And you're not happy till you've got a decent answer, right?

That's good. That means you already think like a scientist. Now you just need to find out more – and to *keep on* asking questions about all the new stuff you discover – and you'll have astronomy and Space science **sorted** in no time. Which is, of course, the point of all this. And to have some fun, naturally.

Now where were we? Oh yeah – the Universe. No sense starting to explore it before we know what it actually *is*, right? So here goes . . .

The Universe is *all there is*. Literally. *Everything*. All of it. It contains everything from vast galaxies, stars and black holes down to planets, moons, oceans, rivers, lakes, land masses . . . plus every single life-form that lives on (or in) them.

All there is? Like, *everything*?
Yep. *Everything*. The word 'universe' comes from the

Greek, meaning 'all together' or 'turned into one'. And as far as we know there's nothing beyond it. Cosmologists reckon it's billions of light years across and, since it's still expanding, it's getting bigger every day. We also know that it's around 13.7 billion years old, and began life in a huge explosion of matter and energy known as the Big Bang. (They must have been up all night thinking up the name for that one.) Before that there was nothing. No matter, no energy . . . no *Space*, even. The Bang created all these things as it went.

GET IT SORTED

A **light year** is the distance travelled by a particle of light, moving at the speed of light, in one Earth year. Since the speed of light is roughly 300 million metres per second (or 670 million miles per hour), that means a light year is roughly equal to about 9,500,000,000,000 kilometres, or 5,900,000,000,000 miles. Or, put another way, 63,000 times the distance from the Earth to the Sun. Now multiply that by 13,700,000,000 and that'll give you some idea of how big the Universe is. That's if your head/calculator/computer hasn't just exploded trying to do it.

We also know that the Universe contains over 100 billion galaxies, within which at least 70,000 million million million (or 70 sextillion) stars happily twinkle. Well, not so much *twinkle* as *burn*.

Stars burn?
Yep. And, what's more, they burn brighter and hotter than anything on Earth. Stars, we've discovered, are not little twinkling dots in the dark curtain of the sky. They are massive, ball-shaped nuclear reactors – giant spheres of hydrogen and helium gas burning and exploding with energy from nuclear reactions going on within them.

Yikes. That sounds a bit scary, actually. Massive nuclear reactors. Like . . . how massive?
Well, our own star – the Sun – is roughly 109 times wider than the Earth, and 330,000 times heavier. And that's not even one of the big ones. Some stars are 100 to 1,000 times wider *again*. They can get so massive, in fact, that they collapse in on themselves, then rebound with an explosion that burns a billion times brighter than the Sun – leaving behind an enormous, invisible hole in Space from which nothing can escape. What's more, a monstrous black hole like this could lie at the centre of our own galaxy, the Milky Way.

GET IT SORTED

Unlike galaxies and solar systems, the Universe has no **single central point**, and may have **no edge**. Physicists say it's quite possible that the Universe simply folds back on itself. So if you flew a spaceship in one direction for long enough, you would never actually reach the edge of the Universe. Just like flying an aeroplane around the world, you'd end up back where you started. Only billions of years older, and probably quite annoyed.

But how do you *know* all this stuff? I mean it's not like you can jet about in Space with a huge ruler, measuring the stars and the distances between them, is it? And if black holes are invisible, how do we know they even *exist*, let alone where they are? Again – great question. The answer is: we use science.

Science isn't just a collection of clever facts and figures. It's a way – an incredibly clever and useful way – of figuring things out using not only careful measurements, but also theories, tests and experiments. So while astronomers can't string tape measures across stars and between galaxies, they can measure the light that comes from them, using telescopes and other instruments. Believe it or not, they can then use that light (together with some scientific theories and a bit of maths) to figure out all sorts of things about the thing it came from. Like how large, how far away and what kind of star it is. Often, they can even tell what it's made of and how old it is – all from one tiny speck of light! Like police detectives working with tiny scraps of evidence, scientists can piece together an entire story from bits and pieces that seem to mean nothing.

How about this?

Early Greek astronomer and mathematician Erastosthenes (276–195 BC) successfully calculated the width and circumference of the Earth, the tilt of the Earth's axis and the distance from the Earth to the Sun, all without telescopes or other modern scientific instruments.

His crack at the Earth's circumference was 250,000 stadia, or about 39,700 kilometres. The real figure, we now know, is around 40,000 kilometres. Not too shabby for a scientist working 2,000 years ago!

Hmmm. So science is like detective work? Never thought of it like that before . . .
Right. And that's what makes science such an exciting and powerful thing to learn about. It's not just a collection of facts to be learned. It's a method. And you can use it yourself to find out more about the world around you, just as working scientists do every day. We'll be doing plenty of that, and discovery and detective work right here.

So where do we start?
We'll kick off with a look at astronomy itself. We'll see when and where it began, and how it developed from simple stargazing and fortune-telling to a science that has allowed us to send men to the Moon, roving robots to Mars and Space

probes to Saturn and beyond.

Then we'll see what astronomers have discovered – all the exciting and cool stuff they've found out about stars, galaxies, solar systems and more. From there, we're off on a whirlwind tour of our own solar system, complete with planets, moons, comets and asteroid belts. We'll learn what Saturn's rings are made of, why Uranus rolls sideways around the solar system and why poor old Pluto doesn't get to be a planet any more.

All this whizzing around the planets should whet your appetite for the last section, on travelling and living in Space, where we'll look at spaceships, Space exploration, Space stations and Space colonies on other worlds. Finally, we'll take a look at what lies beyond the outer reaches of our solar system. We'll join the search for alien life, puzzle over the mystery of the sinister and invisible Dark Matter that fills the Universe, and have a guess at what might happen to the Universe in the far distant future.

If that sounds like fun to you, then grab your Space boots and star map, as we're off to get Space **SORTED!**

2.
From Stargazing to Star Science

What's the difference between astronomy and astrology?

*They both involve looking at the stars, but there the similarity pretty much ends. Astronomers study the stars to increase our knowledge of the Universe. Astrologers use them to predict the future. And although astrology came first, and for a time they developed side by side, astronomy is a science, whereas astrology is definitely **not**.*

So how far back does all this stargazing go?

You might be surprised to find out that the roots of astronomy go waaaaay back, and that people all over the world have been star-gazing since ancient times.

But how did they do it without telescopes and instruments and stuff?

Well, we'll get to that in a minute. But basically they started by just looking at the stars, and spotting patterns in the sky that would tell them things.

Like what kind of week they were gonna have, who they would meet and stuff like that? Like reading the 'stars' in the paper? My mum does that.

Ah. Not quite. That's not really *astronomy*, you see – that's *astrology*.

Are they really that different?
Yes, they are.

In ancient times, astrology and astronomy developed alongside each other. But these are now two very different things, and one sure way to annoy astro**nom**ers is to call them astro**log**ers by mistake. Astronomers observe the stars, planets and other **celestial objects** to learn more about the Universe and how it works.

Astrologers, on the other hand, view the stars and planets as fortune-telling signs – like tea-leaves, or palm lines – and use them to draw up horoscopes and predict the future. Whether or not you believe astrology works is up to you. But, since no one has ever proved whether it works or not, you can't call it a science. That's the big difference between science and non-science. Science demands more than just **looking**, **measuring** and coming up with **explanations**. It also asks us to **prove** our ideas. Or, at the very least, **test** them over and over again to make sure they're not way off . . .

GET IT SORTED

Celestial objects are objects found outside the Earth's atmosphere, such as galaxies, stars, planets, moons and comets. They're usually viewed in the night sky, though some are also visible during the day.

Astronomy is the scientific study of celestial objects and Space, which uses careful observations and theories of physics, chemistry and mathematics to explain how the Universe works.

Astrology is a non-scientific practice which centres around the belief that the movement of rocks and gas balls in Space directly affects the personal lives of people on Earth. So, if Venus moves between the Earth and a certain group of distant stars, then 'love waits behind a green door (possibly wearing a black hat)'. If Mars and Mercury line up, it's 'a bad day to travel'. And so on.

Astrology, in one form or another, has been practised on almost every continent in the world, and by most of the world's many cultures. The Aboriginal Australians, the Native American Indians, the Inuits and the ancient tribes of Europe, Africa and Mongolia all had (or still have) their own methods of tracking the stars and planets, and their own explanations for what their shapes and movements mean.

So they didn't all see the same stars?

Well, they *were* the same stars they were looking at, and many of them even recognized the same star patterns (or **constellations**) as each other. But they *called* them different things. To the ancient Egyptians, the constellation we now know as **Orion** (the Hunter)

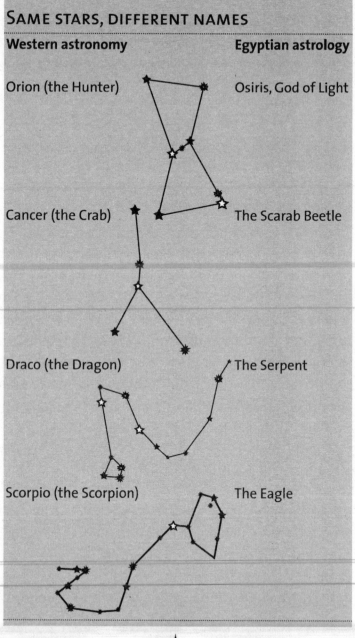

SAME STARS, DIFFERENT NAMES

Western astronomy   **Egyptian astrology**

Orion (the Hunter)   Osiris, God of Light

Cancer (the Crab)   The Scarab Beetle

Draco (the Dragon)   The Serpent

Scorpio (the Scorpion)   The Eagle

was **Osiris** (the God of Light). Other cultures saw it as a giant turtle or octopus. Which just goes to show you that it depends who's looking as I can't quite see the octopus myself . . .

But why did they bother with all this? I mean, looking at stars is fun and stuff, but what was the point? Different cultures did it for different reasons, and some stargazing systems were more accurate and useful than others. The ancient Maya of South America used theirs to predict solar eclipses. This is when the moon moves between the Sun and the Earth, turning day into night for a few minutes while it passes. The superstitious Maya believed this to be a sign of an angry sky-god, and their high priests and astrologers used this fear as an excuse for going to war. If they sacrificed their captured enemies at the holy temple, the astrological bigwigs explained, the sky-god would be pleased with the offering and bring back the Sun. If they didn't do this, the Sun might never return.

What? But that's just daft! Of course the Sun would come back.
Right you are. And the high priests and astrologers knew that it would come back too – with or without the wars and sacrifices. But the loyal tribes and city folk who formed their armies didn't need to know that, and it was a great way of getting them to fight and conquer smaller tribes. Pretty sneaky of them, really.

Where did the first astronomers come from?

Lots of cultures helped to develop it. The ancient Babylonians, Egyptians and Greeks had perhaps the first advanced stargazing systems, while in the Middle Ages scholars in Asia and the Middle East made huge contributions to astronomy as a modern science.

Wait – what's a Babylonian?
The Babylonians lived over 5,000 years ago in a part of the world which is now known as Iraq.

Oh. Okay. On you go.
They were very skilled mathematicians, and they kept detailed records of sunrises and sunsets that allowed them to construct some of the world's first calendars. Later, the Egyptians charted star constellations and built their magnificent pyramids to line up, at certain times of the year, with the stars' positions in the sky.

Seriously? Wow. That's pretty clever.
Yep. And it gets better. By the first century AD, the ancient Greeks were coming up with models of how the Sun, Moon, planets and stars moved around. And while they weren't quite right – more about that in a minute – they did pave the way for better attempts (and more accurate models) later on. Meanwhile, Chinese astronomers were creating some of

the world's first whole-sky star maps, and keeping measurements accurate enough to build clocks, predict eclipses, track comets and more.

So did they just figure all this stuff out for themselves?

Yes and no. While the ancient Babylonians and Egyptians probably kicked it all off, the Greeks borrowed and improved upon their ideas. And, later still, the Arabs gathered together works from ancient Greece and China and added knowledge of their own. Not many people know it, but we owe much of our astronomical knowledge to the Arab peoples.

The astronomical Arabs

In the Islamic world, the tribes and peoples had their own long history of stargazing. This was, at first, partly for navigating the deserts where they lived (which had few landmarks on the ground, but countless ones overhead in the cloudless, starry skies). But later it was for judging the right time and direction to face for Islamic prayer times.

The Islamic scholars translated ancient Greek writings, and adapted their ideas and instruments to produce calendars and star-charts of their own. Scholars like **Abd Allah Muhammad Ibn Jabir Sinan al-Battani** wrote and rewrote many important works on astrology, and started to draw out the differences between astro**logy**, used for fortune-telling, and astro**nomy** as a pure and accurate study of 'the heavens' for its own sake. It was this idea – and these works – that went on to influence the European scholars who later popularized astronomy as a modern science.

But to see how all that happened we'll have to go back a bit. Back to the Greeks and their groovy models of the Universe . . .

Why did people think the Sun went around the Earth? Were they stupid or something?

*For a while, an Earth-centred solar system was easier to imagine and seemed to make more sense. After all – the Sun and Moon **seemed** to move across the sky and around the Earth, and the Earth didn't **seem** to be moving through Space, so **why not** put it in the middle?*

These days, astronomers know a lot about Space, stars, solar systems and planets. You probably know quite a bit about them yourself. Let's find out.

Have a look at the four sentences below, and think about how you would respond to hearing them.

1) The Sun is in the middle of our solar system.
2) The Earth and all the other planets move around it.
3) The Earth also spins or rotates on its own axis, making one full turn per day.
4) This makes the Sun, Moon and stars seem to rotate or move across the sky.

Now – what was your response to each one?
    Was it:

a) No way. Don't believe you.
b) Really?? I had no idea . . .
c) *Duhhhhhh*. Tell me something I *don't* know.

Duhhh. Everyone knows the Earth goes around the Sun. So (c).

Right. Almost everyone these days would answer (c). All this seems pretty obvious to us now.

But it wasn't *always* that way. In fact, just a few hundred years ago, it seemed pretty obvious to most people (scholars and other clever folks included) that:

1) **The Earth is in the middle of the solar system (and the entire Universe).**
2) **The Earth stays put in Space, and doesn't move at all.**
3) **It doesn't rotate, either.**
4) **The Sun, Moon, planets and stars all circle around the Earth. Roughly once per day.**

But that's just stupid! Weren't very clever, these scholars, were they?

Well, all this might seem strange (or just plain daft) now. But if you think about it these ideas kind of make sense.

Eh?

After all, each day, the Sun rises in the east, moves across the sky, and sets in the west. So does the Moon – although we can't always see it doing so. And if you watch the stars at night for long enough you'll notice that they seem to move too. If you know how to find Polaris, the pole star (and if you don't, I'll tell you how in the next chapter), you might notice that the stars seem to circle around that. (Although you'd have to stay up all night to see them make it even halfway round. And there are more interesting things to watch if you're into stargazing, as we'll soon see.) So it really *looks* like everything is circling us, and that we're staying still.

And if you really think about it, unless someone *told* you the Earth was spinning and circling, why would you think it was?

Errr . . . I'm not following you. What do you mean?

Think about it. You can't *feel* the Earth moving. So where's your evidence for it?

If the Earth is spinning round once per day, then that means everyone in Europe, America and Japan is currently circling the centre of the Earth at about 600 mph. (People in countries nearer the equator are doing close to 1,000!) And if the entire planet circles the Sun once per year that means it's travelling through Space at over 67,000 mph. And yet there's no *whoosh* of air rushing past us in the other direction. Our hair stays unruffled and our

WHOOOOOOH!

clothes (thankfully) aren't blown right off our bodies. There are no signs that we're moving at all.

Hmmm. Now that I think about it . . . you're right.

And this is roughly what people argued for most of astronomical history. And part of the reason why few people believed that the Earth went round the Sun (and not the other way around) until about 400 years ago.

People believed that? For that long?

Yep. *That* long. After the Earth-in-the-middle idea of the solar system was suggested by Aristotle, Ptolemy and other scholars in ancient Greece, the idea stuck around for more than a millennium. While a few people (even in ancient Greece) argued otherwise, they were soon shouted down by other scholars and religious leaders. As a result, almost no one believed in a Sun-centred solar system – right up until the six-teenth century.

Why? What happened then?

It was then that the real battle for the stars would begin. A battle that would change the course of scientific history. And the battleground was Europe.

Are you sitting comfortably? Good. Then let's begin the tale . . .

Star Wars

A long time ago, in a galaxy far, far away . . .

All right, so it wasn't that long ago. And it was . . . well . . . right here. This galaxy. This planet.

Get on with it.

Sorry. Now where was I? Oh, yeah. (Ahem.)

The battle for the stars raged between two camps. On one side, there was the huge army of scholars, religious leaders and ordinary folk who believed that the Earth was in the middle of everything. This is called the **Geocentric** (or 'Earth-centred') model of the solar system. The Middle-Earth army ruled the world from ancient times right up to the late 1500s and beyond.

On the other side were the few philosophers, mathematicians and other scholars who believed that the Earth and other planets circled the Sun. This was called the **Heliocentric** (or 'Sun-centred') model of the solar system. From the 1500s onwards, the Sun-centred

THE EARTH IS THE CENTRE OF THE UNIVERSE!

NO, NO, NO! THE SUN IS THE CENTRE!

rebels started building their numbers, and began their battle to be heard.

But it wasn't easy. As with most wars, each side believed their ideas made the most sense, and neither army was giving up without a fight. Heroes emerged on both sides of the battle, and there are too many to tell of them all. But here are some of the big names and big thinkers who helped to start, fight and settle the argument.

Aristotle: the Earth and the heavens

Aristotle (384–322 BC) was a Greek philosopher and all-round genius. He not only studied and wrote some of the earliest works on astronomy, physics and biology, he was also a musician, a poet and a politician. He set the tone for the whole astronomical argument by offering a clever – and very popular – explanation of how the Sun, planets and stars fit together.

To Aristotle, the Universe was divided into two major bits – the Earth and the heavens. The Earth, where we live, was imperfect and a bit disordered. But the heavens – lofty home of the Sun, the stars, the planets and the gods – were perfect.

Perfect?
Yes. Perfect. Or so Aristotle, and his many followers, believed. He came up with a model of the Universe in which the Earth was surrounded by about 50 rotating (and presumably see-through) spherical shells.

Eh? Bit weird, isn't it?

It is a bit. I suppose it'd look a little like one of those Russian dolls, where smaller shells fit inside bigger and bigger ones. Only instead of dolls picture a multi-sized set of enormous transparent footballs. That should do it.

Anyway, in Aristotle's model, the Earth sat, unmoving, in the very centre. Outside that was the innermost shell (or **celestial sphere**, as he called them) which housed the Moon. This

was somehow lodged into the wall of the invisible shell, so as the shell turned the Moon turned with it. Hence, the Moon went round the Earth, as everyone could clearly see. Made perfect sense to him.

Riiight . . . Perfect sense . . .

Outside that shell or sphere was another one, this time carrying Mercury. The next carried Venus, and the one after that, the Sun. From there, you had spheres carrying Jupiter, Saturn and the 'fixed stars'. And that was it.

But what about the rest of the planets? Like Neptune, and Pluto?
Well, Uranus, Neptune and Pluto hadn't been discovered yet. Astronomers had to wait another 2,000 years, for the invention of the telescope, before anyone could even hope to see those distant planets. And even then it wasn't until 1781 that someone actually spotted Uranus, and another 100 years again until they clocked Neptune. But more about that later. Back to the story.

Pretty and neat as it was, the *real* problem with Aristotle's Universe was that the real planets didn't seem to *behave* the way they were supposed to. The Sun, Moon and stars happily rotated around the Earth more or less as they should have done. But the planets – Mars and Venus, in particular – kept misbehaving. They were often spotted moving 'backwards' through the heavens (something astronomers later called 'retrograde motion') as if their particular celestial spheres had slowed down, sped up or changed direction.

Still – Aristotle's model was as good an explanation as any for how the Universe worked. And, for a while at least, no one could do better. Until, that is, **Ptolemy** hit the scene.

Ptolemy: now here's us in the middle . . .

Claudius Ptolemy (AD 150) came up with a way of explaining those mischievous wandering planets. (As a matter of fact, the word 'planet' comes from the Greek word meaning 'wanderer' – which goes to show you how much of a problem this was.)

So how did he do that? Did he put the Sun in the middle, like where it's supposed to be?

Nope. Ptolemy's model still had the Earth in the middle, but instead of having the planets stuck on simple spheres, he had them moving in **circles on top of circles**. So Mars would orbit a point in Space, which in turn would orbit the Earth. If you followed its path, it looked more like it was looping or bouncing around the Earth than simply lapping it.

PTOLEMY'S HEAD-SPINNING UNIVERSE

Ptolemy solved the 'wandering planet' problem by adding epicycles (or circles on top of circles) to some of the planets' orbits. It sort of worked, but it got pretty twisty and complicated!

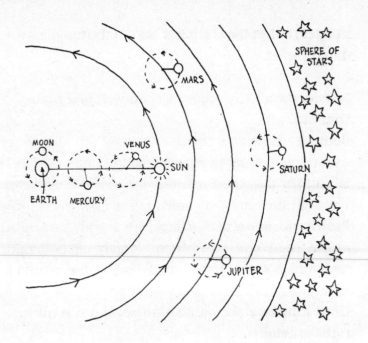

What? Why would anyone believe that? It's so crazy and complicated. It'd never work.

Right. But remember that back then people didn't know any different – or rather didn't have many other ideas to compare it to. What's more, believe it or not, Ptolemy's model more or less *worked*.

It did? But how?

Convinced that circles were the way forward (since Aristotle had stated that the circle was the only shape 'perfect' enough to be in the heavens), Ptolemy used his great mathematical skill to *make* his model work. In truth, it was a lot more complicated than it needed to be, and the real answer to the wandering-planet problem – that the Earth just isn't in the middle – was a lot simpler.

So why didn't the other astronomers just figure that out?

Because Ptolemy's model seemed to fit what astronomers were seeing well enough, and everyone felt happy that the Earth was the *centre of all things*. They felt that this was how it *should* be. Hence, this **Ptolemaic model** of the Universe was widely accepted as the 'right' one, and it stood largely unchallenged for over 1,300 years. (Not at all bad, as theories go.)

Until someone else came along and put it all right . . . right?

Right. It was at this point that the rebels joined the battle in force – led by a Polish astronomer and maths whiz determined to stir up the solar system.

Copernicus: Sun-centred circles

Nicolaus Copernicus (1473–1543) wasn't the first person to suggest the Earth went around the Sun. But thanks to his work many more people became convinced that it *made more sense* that way. He did all the maths, drew all the pictures and wrote an extremely important book arguing for a Sun-centred solar system. His book was called *De Revolutionibus Orbium Celestium*, meaning 'Of the Circling Celestial Spheres'. But his pattern of moving sky-spheres was very different to that of Aristotle.

In Copernicus's solar system, the Sun sat in the middle, with Mercury, Venus, Earth, Mars, Jupiter and Saturn circling around it. The Moon, he said, was alone in circling the Earth, and the 'fixed stars' still sat outside the whole arrangement. Sound familiar? It should, as it's more or less how we know the planets to be arranged, even today.

So everyone went for it, and Copernicus won the battle, right?

Errr . . . not quite. You see, there was a problem with Copernicus's Sun-centred circles. They didn't quite work.

What?!

They didn't even work as well as Ptolemy's complicated circles-upon-circles did.

But why didn't it work? I mean, it was basically right, right? Sun in the middle, planets circling around it? So what was the problem?

Good point. It should have worked, but didn't. Why? Well, it took the intelligence and precision of a German to figure that one out . . .

Kepler: ovals for orbits

Johannes Kepler (1571–1630) was a German mathematician and astronomer who sussed out, amongst other things, the nature of Copernicus's problem.

So what was it?
Basically this: Copernicus was right to argue that the planets circle the Sun, rather than the Earth. But he was wrong in thinking they move in *circles*. Because they don't.

They don't?
Nope. Planets actually orbit the Sun in flattened circles, otherwise known as ovals or **ellipses**. By trying to keep Aristotle's perfect heavenly circles and spheres, Copernicus – like Aristotle – had come up with a beautiful, neat model that the planets simply refused to follow. Once Kepler had figured this out and tried using ellipses *instead* of circles, everything started falling into place.

His Sun-centred, oval-orbit model of the solar system didn't just work better than those of Ptolemy and Copernicus – it worked perfectly. Kepler even figured out how to calculate the path and speed of each planet's orbit based on how far it was from the Sun.

His three Laws of Planetary Motion, which tell us how to do this, still stand today.

LOOPY PLANETS

Kepler's Laws show us how planets move in their oval orbits – speeding up as they slingshot around the Sun, then slowing down on the outward journey.

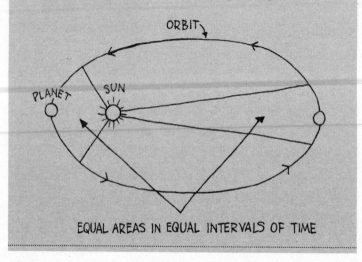

EQUAL AREAS IN EQUAL INTERVALS OF TIME

So that was it, then? Solar system sorted. Problem solved.

Sadly, no. Not *just* yet.

While Kepler's tweaks to Copernicus's Sun-centred system worked a treat, many (or most) people still refused to believe the Earth wasn't sitting, neat and still, in the centre of the Universe. This was for much the same reasons as always. 'We can't feel the Earth moving', 'the Earth is in the middle of everything – the Bible says so' (even though it doesn't really say that at all) and so on.

So the battle raged on, and still more heroes of astronomy lined up to fight it . . .

Galileo: look, it moves!

Galileo Galilei (1564–1642) was one of those heroes, and although he didn't win the battle outright, the arguments and evidence he put forward helped tip the odds in favour of the Sun-centred rebellion.

Galileo, an Italian mathematician, philosopher and engineer, built some of the world's earliest (but not the very first) telescopes. More importantly, he was one of the first people to use telescopes to make detailed, accurate observations of the planets and stars. He saw sunspots on the Sun, mountains on the Moon and was puzzled by the 'ears' he spotted on Saturn. (We now know they were Saturn's rings, but he wasn't to know that!)

But what difference did that make?
Not much, at first. But then he turned his telescope on Jupiter. There, Galileo discovered four moons orbiting around it.

So what? So Jupiter had moons. Big deal.
Ahh – but it *was* a big deal. Back then, you see, the

only planet known to have a moon was ours – the Earth. This was one of the arguments the Middle-Earth scholars used to defend their model. 'Everything goes around us,' they argued, 'and nothing goes around anything else. Therefore, we must be the perfect centre of everything.'

But now Jupiter *did* have something going around it. Four things, in fact. Oops. Looks like we weren't the centre of *everything*, after all.

JUPITER'S MULTI-MOONS

Jupiter actually has at least sixty-three moons, most of which were discovered in the last few years! Galileo discovered the first four in 1610, and between then and 1999, ten more were found, bringing the total to fourteen. Then, between 2000 and 2003, astronomers spotted another *thirty-two* moons, and they're still going!

For this and other reasons, Galileo argued that the Sun *was* clearly in the centre of the solar system, and the Earth *did* move around it, just as Copernicus and Kepler had described. And he wrote and published books saying so.

. . . and everyone read them, and *at last* the battle was over. Right?
Errr, no. Sorry.

Argh!! Why not?

Well, for one thing, most people at that time didn't know how to read. For another, Galileo's books didn't go over too well with most religious leaders in Europe. They felt that saying the Earth *wasn't* the perfect centre of everything was blasphemy – like mocking the Bible and God. The Catholic Church arrested and threatened Galileo, and forced him to apologize in public, saying that he lied, and that the Earth doesn't move at all. But in true rebel style, it's said that he mumbled 'nevertheless, it moves' under his breath, right afterwards.

Heh, heh. Nice work. But if he didn't sort it all out, then who did?

Well, no one person sorted the whole thing. But if one guy could take the credit for convincing the most people, it would probably be the famous British hero of science, Sir Isaac Newton.

Newton: here's *why* it moves . . . gravity

Sir Isaac Newton (1642–1727) built on Galileo's groundwork, and delivered what was to be the final blow to the Middle-Earth army. Going far beyond all other models before him, Newton was a mathematical genius who figured out – amongst a gazillion other things – *what makes* planets orbit the Sun. And the answer to that puzzle was **gravity**.

Gravity, said Newton, is a force that attracts everything in the Universe to everything else. And the bigger and closer together any two things are, the more attraction there is between them. Stars, planets and moons are about as big as it gets. So . . .

- we (along with the atmosphere, oceans, trees, three-toed sloths and everything else) are held to the surface of the Earth by the attractive pull of gravity,
- the **Moon** is pulled into orbit around the **Earth** by **their** combined gravitational attraction
- and the Earth is pulled into orbit around the Sun by their combined gravitational force, also.

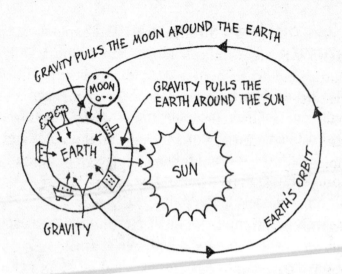

This neatly solved the problem of why we can't feel the Earth moving – the air moves with us, because it's stuck to the Earth too, so it doesn't rush past us as we move through Space. But, more importantly, it also explained why the **smaller planets** would orbit a **larger Sun**, rather than the other way around.

Beyond, this, Newton gave us his Laws of Gravitational Attraction, and his Three Laws of Motion, which allow us to calculate and predict the orbit and motion of almost any object – be it planet, tennis ball, moon or missile – in the Universe. Using his laws and equations, he successfully predicted the positions and motions of all the planets then known to be in the solar system. What's more, a century later, astronomers used the same laws to predict where Neptune *should* be (and found it within hours of turning their telescopes to that point of the sky).

Armed with his theories, laws and explanations, Newton made it difficult for the remaining Middle-Earth scholars to protest. They'd simply run out of reasons. Newton's explanation of the solar system not only told us how it behaved, but also why it behaved that way – because of gravity. Beyond that, his equations predicted precisely where planets would be, and never seemed to be wrong. Hard to top that.

So that was it? Newton nailed it, and now we use his ideas because he's never been topped?
Yes. Well, kind of. While the battle for the shape of the solar system was pretty much won, there was perhaps one more guy who went beyond Newton. Perhaps the most famous scientist in history. Yep – you guessed it. It was Albert Einstein.

Einstein: but what *is* gravity?

Albert Einstein (1879–1955) was a German office worker and amateur physicist when he came up with an idea that would change our view of the Universe once and for all. If anyone can be said to have topped Newton, it's him.

Einstein's work was pure genius, and to tell you everything about what it means would take at least ten more books like this one. But he gets an honorary mention here, because his General Theory of Relativity provided the final evidence for a Sun-centred solar system, and proved once and for all that Copernicus, Kepler, Galileo and everyone else who had argued for it were right all along.

Einstein's work told us not only how gravity works (as Newton's did), but also *what gravity is*. Gravity, said Einstein, is a warping or folding of Space around any object in the Universe. And the more massive the object, the more warping there is.

Eh? But how can Space fold up? I mean, it's . . . well . . . Space. You can't bend it or crumple it. It's just kind of . . . there. Right?

Well, it's pretty hard for us to picture, but Space *does* in fact fold and bend like a sheet. It just does it in four dimensions, instead of the usual three.

Errr . . . four dimensions? You've lost me there.
Einstein believed that three-dimensional Space and the extra dimension of time formed parts of the same thing – a four-dimensional 'fabric' called space-time. Gravity, said Einstein, is a warping of space-time. Try this. Imagine the Sun as a giant basketball placed on a huge, flat sheet (the fabric of space-time), and the planets as tennis balls and golf balls placed alongside it. The weight (or mass) of the ball puts a dent into the sheet, and any object close enough to the dent will roll in, following the warping or curving of the dent around the ball. Roll a golf ball past the basketball, and it'll start rolling in circles around the dent. And that's similar to how planets orbit suns (and moons orbit planets) in Space.

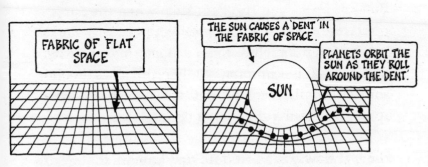

FABRIC OF 'FLAT' SPACE

THE SUN CAUSES A DENT IN THE FABRIC OF SPACE.

PLANETS ORBIT THE SUN AS THEY ROLL AROUND THE DENT.

SUN

Knowing this helps explain why planets would bother to orbit the Sun in the first place (rather than, say, just be pulled straight into it by the force of Newton's famous gravity). So Einstein's bendy space-time helped add another piece to the puzzle of the Sun-centred solar system. But it also gave us something else. It gave us evidence, or proof, that the Earth definitely, positively moves through Space.

Bendy light

Perhaps the most important part of Einstein's theory, for the purposes of our story, is that his warping gravity would not only bend orbiting planets around massive suns, it would also bend **light**. If this were true, Einstein argued, then you should be able to see a tiny shift in the position of a star behind the Sun when the Sun moves between us and that star. The light from it will literally bend around the Sun, and will seem to be in a different spot, relative to the other stars around it.

But – duhhh – you can't see stars when the Sun's out. That means it's *daytime*.
Right. Unfortunately, we can't *usually* see stars close to the Sun (or even anywhere near it), since the Sun shines so much brighter and bounces off the atmosphere, obscuring the fainter light from the stars beyond. *That's* why we can't see stars during the daytime, and why the first ones only appear as the Sun is setting.

See. Told you.

But fortunately there is one time when we can see stars close to the Sun. That's during a solar eclipse.

In an eclipse, the Moon moves between the Earth and the Sun, shading a region of the Earth from its rays, and darkening the skies. Stars are visible during the daytime, and astronomers can look at them – even stars close to the Sun itself.

And that, in 1919, is what scientist and adventurer Sir Arthur Eddington did. He led two expeditions across the world just to be there during an eclipse, so that his team of astronomers could turn their telescopes on to stars near the Sun. When they did so, they noticed just what Einstein had predicted – the stars had shifted. Which meant the light was bent, and Einstein's Space-bending gravity was real.

Hooray! *Finally*. Victory to the rebels!

Yep. Finally. By this time, as I said before, the battle was pretty much already over. Most people had long since accepted the Sun-centred solar system, and Newton's theories of gravity and gravitation. But Einstein's work nailed it once and for all. We not only knew what the Universe looked like, and how it behaved, we also knew *why* it behaved that way.

And somewhere along the way real, proper science was born.

How the war was won

You see, without science or a scientific method, we could still be arguing about all this now. Very few of us get the chance to actually go up to Space and see the Earth from the outside. So we can't just nip up there and check for ourselves which model of the solar system is correct.

What's more, even those lucky few astronauts and cosmonauts who *have* been up there haven't yet made it any further than the Moon. So *nobody* has got far enough away to leave the solar system, turn around and see it how it all works from the outside in.

So how do we really *know* how it works? When did science come into it?

The answer to that is easily found in the *Star Wars* story we've just heard. As the battle for the stars raged on, early astrology gradually turned into the *science* of astronomy with the addition of careful observations, accurate measurements, tests and experiments. Without these things, any idea or opinion about how the Universe works would be as good as any other. But *with* them, you've got the makings of a solid **scientific theory**.

Now let's see how modern astronomers put it into action to find out some of the coolest stuff in the Universe . . .

Astronomer word search

Aristotle   Gravity   Ellipse   Newton

Einstein   Kepler   Ptolemy   Orbit

Copernicus   Heliocentric   Geocentric

```
K U S K F Z J H Y C A B N D F V N J K A
X R F C C X C A E G X E T E V G Z E Y H
O R K O T H H P U L U U C S W M B N Q V
L H K Z I D D E O J I B G O O T K H O X
D V K B C I R T N E C O E G O E O N G A
A M D A N T P U S V C Q C H D L L N X A
R S U C I N R E P O C D L E R T P K N S
U F R I E R X D A Y H W F K N O T V R P
U L X O T B J B W M U H V E S T Q W S W
N T W C S W P W J E I X T P N S R I L T
P N H X N I V Y H L O W K L S I V I X Y
Q E Y T I V A R G O X B D E V R I X C O
K M S C E I R B N T I I M R F A I V X D
O D H P K P Z N C P H R N F W S C M B A
B Q J T I F E Z C J U J C P P O M N J O
D L U E O L U X J O H Q H U M Q V T M G
W U U T R N L Z W X E L X Z E Z J V I W
C E J R B F P E U G P H T G Q X S D M I
N X F A I P T A M Q M C B B U E S Q G O
F R V R T B Y J D I X A J D K K C T J I
```

(answers on page 251)

3.
Measuring Stars and Planets

How do astronomers know how big and how far away the planets and stars are? Aren't they, like, waaay too big to measure?

Obviously, astronomers can't very well string a tape measure thousands of miles around the belly of a planet. And you'd need one **trillions** *of miles long to reach between the stars. So, instead, they use careful observations, some cunning knowledge about how light behaves and a lot of maths to figure it all out.*

Nahh – I reckon they just try and blag it. Like, 'Well, Professor, that star looks about 20 million light years off to me. What'cha reckon?'

I suppose they could, but astronomy wouldn't be much of a science if they did. Plus you'd expect them to argue a lot more if it was all based on guesswork. Instead, astronomers all agree that the Earth is about 8,000 miles (or 13,000 km) wide, and that the nearest star to us (besides the Sun, of course) is Proxima Centauri, which lies about 4.2 light years (roughly 62 trillion miles) from Earth. Think about it – it'd be pretty impressive if you asked two people to pick a number, and they both came up with 62 trillion. Well, hundreds of astronomers worldwide have picked that same number for Proxima Centauri again and again. So, somehow, they must know something the rest of us don't.

Okay, so if they don't just look and guess, how *do* they do it?
In short, they look **very carefully**, and measure **all kinds of different things** to make sure their figures **back each other up**. With the right equipment, and the right theories and equations, astronomers can use their careful observations to suss out (or **deduce**) all kinds of things about stars, planets, galaxies and other objects in the night sky. And after all that measuring and deducing, they **test** what they think they know by making even **more** observations.

But stars and planets look the same – like tiny dots in the sky. How do astronomers know which is which?
Well, we'll be coming to that in the next section. But here's a quick, rough-and-ready guide to get you started with identifying objects in the night sky:

Stars
- Twinkle
- Are relatively dim
- Don't seem to move as you look at them

Planets
- Don't really twinkle
- Are relatively bright*
- Don't seem to move as you look at them

Satellites
- Don't really twinkle
- Are relatively bright
- Often move quickly in a straight line across the sky as you watch them

Aeroplanes and helicopters
- Don't twinkle (but may blink on and off in a regular pattern)
- Are very bright
- Move slowly across the sky as you watch them

Cool! But how does that work? I mean – why don't planets move?

Stars and planets **never seem to move** against the

---

* If, that is, you're looking at Venus, Mars, Jupiter or Saturn. Uranus and Neptune are pretty much invisible to the naked eye, while Mercury lies so close to the Sun that it gets *outshone*, and is only clearly seen at sunrise or sunset during a **solar eclipse**. There's more about planets and eclipses later on.

background of other stars (at least not that you can tell) because they're so far away. It's a bit like looking out of a train window at the landscape as you pass by. Trees and buildings close to the tracks seem to whip past you very quickly. But the further out you look, the slower they seem to go, and objects on the horizon hardly seem to move at all. To stargazers looking up into Space from a fast-moving Earth, distant stars and planets appear much the same way – only they're *so far* away that they appear motionless to the naked eye. So if it looks like it's moving, it's likely to be something a lot closer to Earth – like a satellite in orbit, or an aircraft well within the atmosphere. Near-earth objects like satellites and aircraft also tend to be **much brighter** than distant stars and planets.

Okay, so what about the twinkling?

Stars **twinkle** because their points of light (coming from far outside our solar system) is more easily blurred by the movement of gases in the Earth's atmosphere. Planets **don't** twinkle so much, as their light is a steady reflection of light from our nearby Sun.

Of course, this guide isn't a hundred per cent accurate. A few stars and galaxies may appear brighter than most of the planets. And it still leaves lots of questions unanswered.

Like what?

Well, if it's a planet, we still don't know *which* planet it is (although if you're looking without a telescope in the middle of the night, it's unlikely to be anything other than Mars, Jupiter or Saturn – more about that later on). And if it's a star we still don't know how big, how hot, how close or how far away it is – let alone whether it's one star, two stars close together (otherwise known as a binary star) or even an entire *galaxy* of stars.

But the point is we've already figured out a whole bunch of stuff just by **looking at the light** coming from a mysterious dot in the sky. And that's pretty much what astronomers do for a living.

Whoa. That's pretty cool, I s'pose.

This also means that to be a good astronomer you have to be an *expert* on light.

How do astronomers figure out so much about stars just by looking at them?

Astronomers and physicists use their knowledge of how light behaves to figure out all kinds of amazing things from fairly simple observations and measurements. Nowadays, complex instruments and computers help them analyze starlight from distant galaxies. But even without equipment, a little knowledge of how light works can go a long way.

Okay, so how complicated can light be? What exactly do they know that we don't?

Well, to tell you everything would take a while. So for those of us who haven't managed to get PhDs in physics or astronomy just yet, here's the short version.

1) Light generally travels in straight lines, from **light sources** to, eventually, our eyes.
2) Light can be bounced (**reflected**) or redirected (**refracted**).
3) Light travels very, very fast, but at a **constant speed**.
4) Visible **white light contains all the colours of the rainbow**, and these colours can be separated out when it bounces off, passes through or is absorbed by an object.

Throughout the rest of this chapter, we'll be looking

at how astronomers use these four simple facts to explore a whole universe of celestial objects – like detectives using light as evidence. And we'll see how you can do some of this detective work too.

A quick question for you: where does light come from?

Errr . . . I dunno. The Sun. The Moon. Lightbulbs.
Right. Sometimes it's from an electric lamp, torch or lightbulb. Sometimes it's from a fire or candle flame. By day it comes from the Sun, and by night from the Moon and stars.

Okay . . . so what?
So all of these things are 'sources' of light. The light rays coming from these things either travels directly to our eyes, or bounces off the objects all around us before reaching our eyes. This is what allows us to see anything at all. It's also the reason why we can't see anything in the dark. When it's dark, there are no light sources around – no candles, no lightbulbs and no Sun or Moon in the sky. With no light sources, there are no rays of light to bounce off the objects around us, and no light rays arrive at our eyes.

Nothing tricky there, right? All pretty obvious.

Duhhhhh. I knew that.
Okay. But to be a good astronomer you have to know the difference between a **true light source** and a

shiny object, which is simply **reflecting** light from somewhere else. To help you spot the difference, here are a few examples.

LIGHT SOURCES	SHINY THINGS
The Sun	The Moon
Stars	Planets
	Comets
	Satellites
	The sky
	The ocean

And here's why:

Stars generate their own light in powerful nuclear fusion reactions that happen deep inside (more on that later). These reactions release light, heat and other forms of radiation into the space around them. A sun is simply a star surrounded by one or more planets, and a galaxy is a collection or cluster of light-producing stars.

Moons and planets don't actually generate light themselves – they reflect it from a nearby sun. Our Moon, bright as it seems, is just a big shiny sphere that reflects sunlight.

Satellites are just shiny lumps of metal that reflect sunlight. If you can see them at night, it means light is striking them from the Sun, unseen below the horizon.

The **sky** (or atmosphere) reflects light from the Sun during the day, but once the Sun has passed below the horizon, half the Earth falls into darkness as rays of sunlight no longer reach the sky above it.

Similarly, the **ocean** reflects sunlight that passes into its upper layers. At night, no sunlight reaches it, and the ocean turns black (unless partially lit by sunlight reflected off the Moon, of course). Even during the middle of the day, the deep ocean remains pitch black, as sunlight is scattered more and more with increasing depth, and cannot penetrate more than a couple of hundred metres.

Okay . . . so now what?

So now we know that stars **produce** light and everything else in Space simply **reflects** it. And if the light (whether straight from the source or bounced off an object) cannot reach our eyes that means we'll be unable to see the light source, or unable to see the object that reflects it.

So what use is that?

Plenty, as it turns out. With that first simple understanding of how light works, you can do all kinds of things – including plenty of easy do-it-yourself astronomy that you don't even need a telescope for.

No way!

Yes, way. Want to find out how? Then read on . . .

How do astronomers know which star is which?

They navigate the sky in much the same way as we do the land or oceans – using maps, landmarks and coordinates. It can take a little practice, but once you get the hang of it you can hop and measure your way from one constellation to another, even without using fancy equipment.

You mean you can really do astronomy without a telescope or anything?

Yep. Star-spotting without instruments is often called 'naked-eye astronomy'. And while you might not be able to see the shapes of galaxies or the rings of Saturn there are still plenty of cool things you can see and do with your eyes and hands alone. Here's how to go about it.

First, make sure you're in a place where you can actually see the stars. In built-up areas with lots of houses, roads and street lights, most of the stars in the sky will be blotted out by **light pollution** (see below). So, if you live in a town or city, head out into the countryside to do your stargazing. Or, better yet, plan a star-spotting camping trip so that you can stay out all night. Once you're clear of the light pollution, hey presto – thousands of fainter light sources suddenly appear in the sky above. Now the Universe is yours to explore.

GET IT SORTED – LIGHT POLLUTION

You may have noticed that the stars can be easier or harder to see in different places, and at different times. Sometimes, this is simply due to the weather. Thick cloud cover on a spring night may leave you unable to see the stars at all. This is because light from the Moon and the ground is reflecting off water droplets in the clouds, stopping you from seeing the night sky beyond. But even on cloudless nights the sky can seem darker – and the stars brighter and more numerous – when viewed from some places, compared with others. And that's usually down to light pollution.

We already know that stars are true light sources. But they're not the *only* light sources around. The electric street lights that shine down on roads and cities by night are light sources too. And, while they're nowhere near as powerful as the stars, they're much, much closer to us. Trillions of miles closer. And the main problem with them is that they don't just *shine down* ... they also *shine up*.

As light radiates and reflects upwards from highways and city streets, it bounces around in the atmosphere above us, turning the very air into a reflecting light source of its own. When this happens, the night sky outshines most of the stars, and you'll be lucky if you can see more than ten or twenty dim-looking dots up there. Thankfully, you can get around this by going star-spotting in places where there are fewer ground-based light sources around.

Okay. So I'm outside looking at the sky right now, and it's . . . well . . . pretty *big*. What should I be looking at?

Well, first filter out all the moving objects in the night sky – like moving satellites and aeroplanes. As you now know, these cannot be stars or planets, so we're not interested in those. That done, you're left with a vast blanket of tiny white dots – mostly stars and galaxies, with a few planets and asteroids scattered in between. Now you need a way of navigating the night sky, so that you can locate some major stars and constellations.

So how do you do that? Do you use a map or a compass or something?

Sort of, yes. Just as map-makers divide up the surface of the Earth using gridded lines of latitude and longitude, astronomers do the same thing using imaginary lines in the sky. And while geographers (and programs like Google Earth) find places on Earth using coordinates, astronomers use **celestial coordinates** to locate objects in the night sky. And so can you.

Brilliant! So where do we go first?

Everywhere! But our first stop will be the Great Bear.

A star-hopping tour of the sky

Start by finding **Ursa Major**, or the **Great Bear**. This is one of the easiest constellations to recognize, and you almost certainly know its shape already. The seven bright stars in the centre of Ursa Major look a bit like a saucepan, and this part is also known as the **Big Dipper** or the **Plough**.

Got it? Good. From here, we can hop about the sky to find other constellations and major stars.

• Locate the two stars which form the outer edge of the 'pan', and extend an imaginary line up through those two points – as if the pan was crackling and spitting with boiling oil, and a single crispy chip popped out of it. Fizz, crackle, pow! Now track your flying chip upwards through 30 degrees (or three fist-widths), and you'll find the pole star, **Polaris**.

• Polaris also forms the tip of the tail on **Ursa Minor** – the **Little Bear**. Ursa Minor looks (to me) a bit like a kite, with Polaris right at the end of the kite's streaming tail. Head another 30 degrees in the same direction, and you'll find a big 'W' shape. This is the constellation of **Cassiopeia**.

Polaris always sits due north in the sky, so you can use it to navigate without a compass, as sailors and travellers did for thousands of years before compasses and satellite navigation. Because the Earth's axis of rotation points towards Polaris (or, rather, its point in Space), all the other stars seem to rotate around it through the course of a night, while Polaris alone seems not to move in the sky. That's what makes it so useful – because it always lies over the north pole, and it never moves, it's the ultimate landmark. Or . . . errr . . . sky-mark. Whatever.

Named after a beautiful queen in Greek mythology, the story goes that **Cassiopeia** was punished for her vanity by the angry god of the sea, Poseidon. He banished her to the skies, where she would be forced to spend half her time hanging upside down, to learn to be humble once again. This is why, it's said, Cassiopeia sometimes looks like a 'W', and other times more like an 'M'. (In reality, the stars that form Cassiopeia simply rotate around Polaris along with all the others, and it's the 180-degree rotation that flips her upside down. But it's a nice story, and it makes the shape easy to spot and remember.)

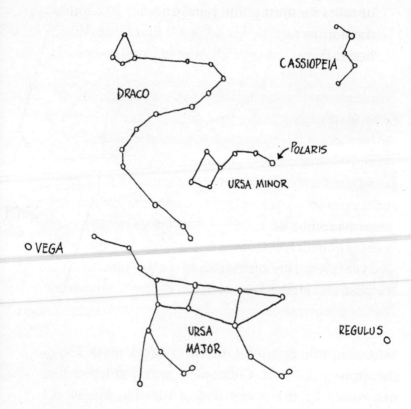

CASSIOPEIA

DRACO

POLARIS

URSA MINOR

○ VEGA

URSA MAJOR

REGULUS ○

- Aside from the 'pan' of Ursa Major, the second best-known constellation in the skies is probably **Orion**, the Hunter. Orion's head, shoulders, legs and belt are easily spotted, and if you look carefully you may also be able to pick out his right arm raised over his head, and his left arm holding a shield (or dead animal, depending on who you listen to!) before him. This shape appears for most of the year in the northern hemisphere.

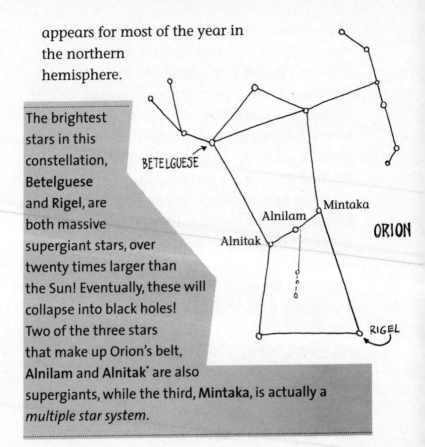

The brightest stars in this constellation, **Betelguese** and **Rigel**, are both massive supergiant stars, over twenty times larger than the Sun! Eventually, these will collapse into black holes! Two of the three stars that make up Orion's belt, **Alnilam** and **Alnitak*** are also supergiants, while the third, **Mintaka**, is actually a *multiple star system*.

- Hanging down from Orion's belt are three stars which form his sword or scabbard. In the centre of these is the Orion Nebula, a massive hydrogen gas cloud over twenty-four light years (or 140 trillion miles) across.

* If you're wondering why all these star names sound strange to you, it's because they come from the Arabic language, having been named by the clever astronomical Arabs we met in the previous chapter.

- Trace a line down and back along the line of Orion's belt, and you'll find **Sirius** – unmistakeable as the brightest star in the night sky. Sirius forms part of the constellation of **Canis Major** – the Great Dog – Orion's faithful hunting companion in the heavens. For this reason, it's also known as the **Dog Star**. It is very bright because it's very big and hot, burning twenty-six times brighter than our own Sun, but also because it's fairly nearby. It's the fifth closest star system to our own, and sits about twice as far from us as the nearest star, Alpha Centauri.

- Finally, to round off our tour, trace a line backwards from Orion's shoulders and you'll arrive at **Procyon**, a very bright star that is actually a binary (or double) star system. Procyon forms one half of **Canis Minor** or **Little Dog** – the Chihuahua of the skies. Procyon, Sirius and Betelguese also form an equilateral triangle, known as the **Winter Triangle**, an easily spotted landmark in the northern hemisphere's winter skies.

Planet-spotting

That just about ties up our first brief trip around the night sky. That's probably about as far as we can go without getting too confused by trying to explore without a complete map of the stars and skies. Of course, with a star map, you can do a lot more. You can locate all eighty-eight of the major constellations, and many more interesting stars and celestial objects. You can also locate the planets – or at least some of them, anyway.

- **Uranus** and **Neptune** are too far away to be seen with the naked eye, and **Mercury** lies so close to the Sun, and is so small and non-reflective, that you can't really see it for more than a couple of weeks out of the year, and even then it's tricky. So of the planets you're *likely* to spot, that leaves **Venus**, **Mars**, **Jupiter** and **Saturn**. (Sorry – **Pluto** isn't a planet any more. We'll find out why in Chapter 5!)
- **Venus**, being close to the Sun, is easily outshone by the Sun itself, and never strays far from the Sun's position in the sky. For this reason, it's only visible at sunrise or sunset – just before the Sun crests the horizon, or just after the Sun has dipped below it.
- **Mars**, **Jupiter** and **Saturn**, however, follow predictable paths across the night skies, which make them more or less visible at certain times of

year. To find these, use a chart or table (like the one in the Appendix) to track their movements by date. Then just look for a non-twinkling object (planets don't twinkle – remember?) in the right place, at the right time.

That's all good fun and, armed with our eyes, hands and a few maps and charts, we can discover plenty of new and exciting astronomical things. But we've now pretty much reached the limit of what we can do with our eyes alone. To do more, and to take our astronomy further, we need to supercharge our eyes. And for that we need some serious gear.

Why do we need telescopes to see distant stars?

Because our eyes aren't big enough to collect the tiny amounts of dim light that radiate from distant objects in Space. Nor are eye lenses powerful enough to magnify and resolve objects trillions of miles away. We use telescopes and other instruments to supercharge our vision – enabling us to see more than we could ever hope to see without them.

So telescopes give us supervision?
In a way, yes.

How do they do that?
The basic idea of the telescope goes back to the early

seventeenth century (although magnifying lenses go waaaay further back – see the next page for a history of the telescope). Telescopes do two main things. Firstly, they **gather more light** than your eyes could manage alone. Secondly, they **focus** that light.

In this way telescopes magnify distant objects, giving larger visible images for us to study. They also allow us to distinguish between close-together objects at a distance (like two stars so close together in the sky that they appear to the naked eye as one), and to see fine details that would otherwise be invisible, like small mounds and impact craters on the Moon. And, in general, the larger the telescope is, the more distant the objects you can see and the more detail you can observe.

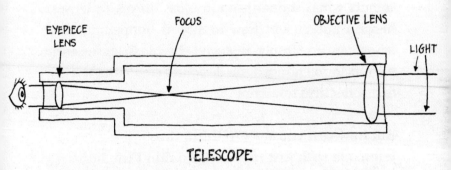

EYEPIECE LENS · FOCUS · OBJECTIVE LENS · LIGHT

TELESCOPE

So did astronomers just keep building bigger and bigger telescopes until they ended up with those massive ones on hilltops?

Not quite. There were limits to how big they could

make glass lenses like this, and to how much they could improve on the images they were seeing through their bigger, longer telescopes. Glass lenses above a certain size sag and bend under their own weight, distorting the light and images viewed through them. And because they also **refract** (or split) white light into different colours, glass lenses create weird blurring and coloured halos around the objects you're trying to look at. So, while glass-lensed **refracting telescopes** worked for a while, it soon became clear that something else was needed. Mirrors.

Mirrors?
Right. Mirrors. Isaac Newton (again, one of those all-round clever blokes from the last chapter) not only figured out why white light splits into different colours when shone through glass prisms or lenses, he also figured out how to stop it happening in a telescope. He simply replaced the glass lenses with mirrors, and changed the design to create the world's first **reflecting telescope**.

But how can you see anything through a telescope with just mirrors? Wouldn't the light just bounce back at the sky?
If you only used one mirror, then yes. But Newton cleverly used two of them, so that the image gets bounced out of an eyepiece at the side (not the end) of the telescope, which the astronomers then peer

into. Although a small central circle of the sky is blotted out by the inner mirror, it's not as much as you might think. And, more importantly, the rest of the image is crystal clear – provided you craft mirrors with the right curves to correctly focus the light. And keep them clean, of course.

So, ever since Newton, telescopes have had mirrors?

Pretty much. The heart of most large telescopes is the light-gathering primary mirror at the base. The biggest have primary mirrors measuring 5 m (200 inches) or more across. But there have also been a few additions to Newton's basic design since then – adding or angling mirrors to produce different effects for different purposes. In a **cassegrain focus** telescope, light is reflected from the inner mirror straight back through a hole in the main one. This increases the focal length (the distance the light travels between the mirrors) giving greater magnification, and allows the astronomer to look straight up along the length of the telescope. In a **prime focus** telescope, the light may bounce just once off the primary mirror, and the astronomer sits *inside* the telescope to make his or her observations.

They sit *inside* it?

Yep. Obviously – since you can't shrink the astronomer – this only works for very large telescopes. But it works

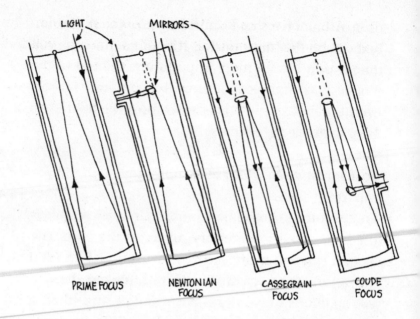

LIGHT MIRRORS

PRIME FOCUS | NEWTONIAN FOCUS | CASSEGRAIN FOCUS | COUDE FOCUS

very well for seeing fine details. In fact, many large observatory telescopes have motorized mirrors that can be moved or tilted to send the light to different focal points. So one telescope may have a **prime focus** inside, a **cassegrain focus** at the end and another (called the **coude focus**) to one side, at right angles to the body of the scope.

So there are chairs and eye-holes at each of these spots, and the astronomer can choose where to sit and view from?

Sometimes. But sometimes there may not be a person there at all. Instead of an astronomer, there may be a remote-controlled digital camera taking pictures, or a cache of computers and instruments analyzing both the visible light or invisible radiation entering the telescope.

Invisible radiation? Yikes. That sounds a bit scary.

Not really. In fact many modern telescopes aren't even designed for 'looking' at the visible light coming from stars. Instead, they search patches of Space for objects emitting invisible radiation – like infrared, ultraviolet, x-rays and gamma rays.

They spend all day looking at invisible stuff? Weird.

Trust me – it gets even weirder. They also use telescopes to search for objects in the sky.

Lots of celestial objects (like stars, galaxies, pulsars and black holes) also give off **radio waves**, and some of the biggest discoveries in modern astronomy have been made using **radio telescopes** rather than **optical** (or light-detecting) ones.

Smart! So can I search for new galaxies and stars using my radio or satellite dish at home?

Well, you can try, but unfortunately you're unlikely to have much success, since radio telescopes generally have to be pretty big to be of any use. Because radio waves are much harder to gather and focus than visible light radiation you need a massive dish (or a whole set of large dishes) to gather, focus and detect them. The world-famous Arecibo Observatory in Puerto Rico, for example, uses a radio telescope with a dish over 305 m (1,000 feet) across.

Meanwhile, in the New Mexico desert, the imaginatively named **Very Large Array** (or **VLA**) features a set of twenty-seven dish antennas – each 25 m (80 feet) wide – spaced out across the desert and pointed in the same direction to search for objects in the sky.

Pah. I'll never fit one of those in my garden.
No. Probably not.

So what about Hubble and all those Space telescopes we hear about so much? Are they massively enormous ones too?
Not really. Hubble is a large optical telescope, but it has a pretty small primary mirror as reflecting telescopes go. The big deal about Hubble is that it sits outside most of the Earth's atmosphere, in a low orbit of the planet, taking pictures of deep Space that are unclouded by the shifting, reflecting gases other telescopes have to peer up through. (Most of the big Earth-based optical telescopes are planted in high-altitude observatories, to try and get above the clouds and atmospheric pollution. But even they have to look up through a layer of gases several miles thick that Hubble lies smugly beyond.) For this reason, Hubble

has captured some of the clearest and most beautiful images of deep Space objects ever seen – despite being a relatively small (and elderly) telescope.

Elderly?

Yep. Hubble was launched in 1990 and only designed to run for about ten years, but after a few repairs, cleanings and mirror-replacements it's now approaching its twentieth birthday – and still going strong! In a few years, NASA's set to trump this with the James Webb Space Telescope. The JWST has a larger mirror, shielded from solar radiation, and detectors for infrared and other types of radiation Hubble can't see. With this, astronomers are hoping to get all-new views of the Universe, and an all-new understanding of how it all works.

Thanks to many years of observations and data from optical, radio and Space telescopes, astronomers have already figured out a huge amount about stars and galaxies – including how they're born, why they develop into different shapes and sizes, and how they interact with each other across the reaches of Space.

. . . And that's what we're off to find out next.

4.

The Secret Life of Stars and Galaxies

How do we know that stars and galaxies are billions of years old, if there were no people around billions of years ago to see them?

Looking deep into Space at distant stars and galaxies is like looking back in time. Astronomers use that fact to figure out how old certain stars and galaxies must be, and also to figure out how they develop and grow.

Hang on – *what*? If stars and galaxies are supposed to be billions of years old, then how can we know anything about how they're born, or how they grow? I mean, we weren't even around billions of years ago to look up at them, let alone use telescopes and science . . . right?

That's true. The human race is only about 100,000 years old, whereas most of the stars and galaxies we see in the night sky are millions or billions of years old. But when we look deep into Space, light years away from the Earth, we are also – in a way – looking back in time.

Eh? How's that, then?

Well, if you think about it, if the star we're looking at is four light years away, then the light from it has taken four years to travel to the Earth. So we're actually looking at the star *the way it was four years ago*, rather than *the way it is now*. If the star is 1,000 light years away, then its light has taken 1,000 years to get here, and we're seeing the star roughly the way it was when William the Conqueror invaded England in 1066! So looking deep into Space using powerful telescopes is like taking snapshots of the distant past. And by taking a number of snapshots like this – of different stars and galaxies, of different ages, at different stages of development – astronomers can piece together a timeline of how stars and galaxies develop. It's a little like arranging the frames in a cartoon strip to create one complete story.

If galaxies are huge clouds of stars, why can't we see them in the sky?

Because they're so far away that they look like single dots. Unless, that is, you have a telescope. Then you may be able to make out their fuzzy, blobby or spiral shapes. For years, astronomers didn't know what to make of these 'strange, fuzzy stars'. But now we know what they really are: impossibly vast clusters of billions of stars, spinning away in Space.

Is that true? They thought they were fuzzy stars?

They didn't know *what* to think. For many years, astronomers looked into the night sky and saw only stars and the fuzzy, star-like objects we now know to be galaxies. But because astronomers used to think all of these stars and objects were roughly the same distance away from the Earth ('fixed' stars found upon the celestial spheres we saw in Chapter 2), they thought these strange blobs and spirals were simply star-sized gas clouds, or **nebulae**. While in reality they were of course vast clusters of stars many times further away than the stars they seem to lie alongside.

So how did they figure that out?

For a while, they couldn't. For decades, arguments raged about what these 'spiral nebulae' might really be. And then the brilliant astronomer Edwin Hubble sorted it out by using a huge new observatory telescope to pick out individual stars within the spirals. The world's astronomers were forced to recognize that these were not nebulae at all, but vast galaxies of stars, floating in Space at incredible distances from the Earth. And for the first time we realized that our own solar system must be part of a similar cluster of stars, in our own patch of Space.

Although we've never seen it from the outside, we now know our place to be on the outer arm of a spiral galaxy we call the Milky Way – our own galaxy being just one of *billions* of others spread throughout the Universe.

Billions? Whoa . . .

And that's not all. Hubble also made an educated guess – using a method developed earlier by fellow American astronomer Henrietta Leavitt – at how far away some of these galaxies were, based on the brightness of special, pulsating stars within them called **Cepheid Variables**. Using Leavitt's clever mathematical method, he began a catalogue or map of stars and galaxies, complete with distances, which astronomers continue to use to this day.

Is that why they named that big Space telescope after him?

Yep – right you are. The Hubble Space Telescope was named after Hubble partly because of its main mission – to spot and measure new (and previously unseen)

Cepheid Variables, and use them to find the range of even more stars and galaxies. So far, Hubble (the telescope, not the man) has discovered over 800 new Cepheid Variables*, and has measured the distance to over twenty known galaxies.

Wow. He must have been pretty happy with that.
Sadly, Edwin Hubble died in 1953, so never got to see his telescope namesake built or launched. But the work he did changed the face of astronomy forever, and still continues to this day. Since Hubble's death, other astronomers have figured out different ways to calculate ranges to distant stars and galaxies too. And they're using these to put even more stars and galaxies on the map. We might not be able to visit other stars and galaxies yet (we'll see why in Chapter 6), but when we finally do we'll have a good idea which ones to aim for – thanks to Hubble and his ever-growing map of the Universe.

And thanks to Hubble and the many astronomers who have painstakingly continued his work we now know lots more about what stars and galaxies actually *are*, including how they're born, how galaxies of different shapes develop and even how they collapse or 'die' . . .

---

* Polaris, the pole star we met in Chapter 2, is an example of a Cepheid Variable star. It is also believed to be a binary star, orbiting around another companion star nearby. So think about that the next time you spot it!

Where do stars and galaxies come from?

Galaxies are huge clusters of stars that form particular shapes, depending on the numbers, ages and types of stars within. Stars, on the other hand, are basically huge balls of gas and dust held together by the force of gravity. They're formed as massive gas-and-dust clouds are pulled together under their own gravitational attraction, which triggers a series of reactions and transformations that eventually result in a star.

Wait a second – gravity? What gravity? I thought there wasn't any gravity in Space . . .

Ah, but there is. Gravity is *everywhere* in the Universe. It's just that its pull gets weaker the further away you are from the objects (like planets and stars) that produce it. In fact, **every object in Space with mass** (even a tiny speck of dust or gas molecule) **produces gravity** – washing the entire Universe with overlapping gravitational waves from all directions. So although you might hear people talking about 'zero-gravity' conditions up in Space, it's more accurate to say 'micro-gravity', since there's always *some* gravity about.

All right, then – so where did all that dust and gas come from in the first place?

Most is from the remnants of other stars which have long since burned out or exploded. But some –

including the very oldest stars in the Universe – were formed directly from material left over from the Big Bang. In any case, the stuff that goes into making a star is mostly hydrogen gas, together with smaller amounts of helium and other elements. Once enough hydrogen and other molecules have been drawn together by gravity, they are crushed together at immense pressures, and the molecules start to break apart as the immense cloud collapses in on itself. This creates huge amounts of heat and pressure, and eventually results in a huge ball of rotating gas in Space, known as a **protostar** – kind of like a baby star waiting to be born.

Hang on a minute – how does that happen? I mean, I've got dust and gas floating about in my house. Does that mean it could all squish together and form a baby star in my living room? Well, that's pretty unlikely. But not because your dust and gas are not 'star stuff' (in fact, all the dust and gas on the Earth were once part of a nearby star). The main reason a protostar doesn't form spontaneously from the gas and dust in your house is that there's simply *not enough of it*. The **molecular clouds** that form new stars contain truly *immense* amounts of stuff. If you could suck one of these clouds up into some kind of giant gas container, you'd find that a single star-forming cloud would weigh thousands (or even tens of thousands) of times more than our own

Sun. (And since the Sun weighs over 300,000 times as much as the Earth, that's not lightweight, either!)

So get enough stuff in any one place in Space, and it'll collapse to form a baby star?
Basically, yes.

Then what happens? How does the baby star get born?
Once enough heat and pressure build up inside the giant gas ball, the hydrogen atoms within start to fuse and turn into heavier elements. Billions of tonnes of hydrogen atoms fuse to create atoms of deuterium, helium and other elements, releasing massive amounts of energy as they do so. This energy fuels still *more* fusion reactions, and produces *even more* energy in the form of heat, light and other forms of radiation. With this, it becomes a self-sustaining fireball, and the star has truly been born. In the course of a few million years, a vast floating dust cloud has turned into a massive ball-shaped nuclear furnace in Space – otherwise known as a star.

Weird. Then what happens? Does it just keep on burning forever?
Nope. Like everything else in the Universe, stars are born, grow up, grow old and eventually die – or at least pass on into another form. Gas clouds of different sizes form stars of hugely different sizes, types and

temperatures. These burn away in Space for a long (but limited) time. Then eventually they will collapse, explode, or burn out. Which is what we're about to look at next . . .

GET IT SORTED – WEIGHT VS MASS

Physicists and mathematicians often use the terms **weight** and **mass**, which can get pretty confusing if you're not sure what they really are. So, before we go much further, here's the lowdown on mass, density and all things massive:

Mass is basically the **amount of matter** (or stuff) **an object is made of**.
Mass isn't quite the same as weight, which also involves the pull of gravity. Basically, the weight of an object is equal to its mass (m) multiplied by the local pull of gravity (g), or . . .

$$\text{Weight} = (m \times g)$$

At the Earth's surface, the pull of gravity is 1g, so for any object on Earth . . .

$$\text{Weight} = m \times 1$$

. . . which means down here, mass and weight are the same. An object with 10 kg mass weighs 10 kg. End of story.

But on other planets and up in Space the value for the pull of gravity (g) can change, so while a person with a **mass** of 100 kg **weighs** 100 kg on Earth, on the surface of the Moon (which only generates a sixth of the Earth's gravity), they would have a **mass** of **100 kg**, but only **weigh 16.6k g** (100 x 1/6).

So even if your **mass stays constant**, your **weight can change**, depending on where you are. Technically, mountain climbers on the top of Mount Everest weigh a little less than they do at sea level – because they're 8,800 m (or 29,000 feet) further from the centre of the Earth!

How long does a star live for?

It depends how big it is. The smallest embryonic stars can't even get their nuclear fusion reactions kicked off, and fizzle into charred, lifeless lumps called **black dwarfs**.

Slightly bigger **red dwarf** *stars – weighing about half as much as our Sun – may exist for trillions of years in the same state before finally collapsing into faint, dense* **white dwarf** *stars, in which no more nuclear fusion reactions take place, either. Over time, these gradually lose their remaining heat to the surrounding Space, and end their lives as lifeless black dwarf stars.*

That's a bit sad.

A little bit, yes. But you'll be happy to hear that most stars go through many more exciting changes as they grow and develop. Larger **dwarf**, **giant** and **supergiant** stars may spend millions or billions of years burning off their outer layers, then expand, collapse, evolve into new forms, and then repeat the cycle all over again before eventually reaching old age as white dwarfs, and theoretically* ending their lives as black dwarfs.

Do all these stars have planets around them, like our Sun?

---

* We say 'theoretically' because we have never actually *found* a black dwarf. Stars take so long to die like this that the Universe isn't yet old enough for any to have formed. But that's how astronomers think most stars will end up.

Some form part of a solar system – surrounded by planets, moons and other objects – but others do not. Some stars are alone in Space, or orbit one or more **companion stars**, with no planets around them at all. A few types of star – the very biggest ones – literally self-destruct at the end of their lives, in a massive stellar explosion called a **supernova**. Some of these (more on this later) then turn into famously mysterious and deadly **black holes**. But most form part of a **family** of stars, ranging from small and cool to large and hot, with a range of types in between.

Stars have *families*?
Yep. Big ones.

Star families are classed by *temperature* and further sorted by *brightness* (known to astronomers as **magnitude**). There are seven basic classes, which also correspond to certain ranges of size, temperature and colour. This happens because the biggest stars also have the hottest atmospheres, and the hottest stars burn with different colours to the cooler ones. To understand this, just think about heating up a piece of metal in a fire or forge. Just as the metal changes colour when you heat it – from 'red hot' to 'white hot' – a 'cool' star burning away in Space will produce a reddish glow, while hotter stars will produce an orange, yellow, whitish or bluish light, depending on the temperature their atmospheres reach.

THE CLASSES LOOK LIKE THIS:

Class	Size (compared to the Sun)	Temperature	Colour
O	>16 times bigger	>30,000K*	Blue
B	2 – 16 times bigger	10,000–30,000K	Bluish-white
A	1.5 – 2 times bigger	7,500 – 10,000K	White
F	1 – 1.5 times bigger	6,000 – 7,500K	Yellowish-white
G	About the same	5,200 – 6,000K	Yellow
K	Half to 0.8 times	3,700 – 5,200K	Yellowish-orange
M	Less than half	<3,700K	Orange or red

Now if you measure the brightness and colour of as many stars as you can, and put the results on a graph with colour (or temperature) across the bottom, and

---

* 'K' means 'degrees Kelvin'. Kelvins are units of temperature used by astronomers and physicists, equal in size to degrees Celsius, but the scale starts at the lowest temperature you can get, -273°C, or **absolute zero**. To get from K to °C, all you have to do is subtract 273. But since these temperatures are so huge to begin with, there's not much point, and you can think of them as being 'about the same, to the nearest 1,000 degrees'!

magnitude (or brightness compared to the Sun) up the side, an interesting thing happens. The stars start to *form patterns* or *lines* across the graph, with over 90 per cent of all of them falling within one diagonal line from top left to bottom right. This line is known as the **main sequence**, and it tells us that the vast majority of stars in the Universe exist as a single family of steadily evolving stars. The rest – from the tiniest dwarf stars to the largest giant and supergiant stars – form smaller families outside of the main star 'clan'.

Stars *evolve* too? Like, they grow legs and stuff?
Not quite. Although that would be fun to see . . .

Unlike animal evolution (which happens over *generations* of animals), stellar evolution happens within the lifetime of a single star. It describes the process by which a star begins life in one form, and then spends its life evolving or transforming into other star types. For most of its life, a star will live within the range of main sequence stars. But eventually it will leave the sequence by transforming into a super-massive giant or supergiant star, or into a super-dense neutron or white dwarf star. How it lives and ends its life depends on how much material goes into the star in the first place (and, occasionally, on how much it gains or loses from other objects nearby).

Our Sun, for example, is a pretty average **class G yellow dwarf** star, with a mass of around 1.99 x

10^{30} kg (roughly 330,000 times the mass of the Earth), and an average surface temperature of around 6,000K (close to 6,000°C, or 11,000°F). It started life around 4.5 billion years ago, and will probably remain as a yellow dwarf (a typical main sequence star) for another 5 billion years. So it's more or less middle-aged!

So what happens after that?
In 5 billion years' time, it will have burned through most the hydrogen and helium in its core. When that happens, the core will begin to shrink while the outer layers expand and cool, turning the Sun from a hot yellow dwarf into a larger (but cooler) **red giant** star.

How much larger will it be then?
Right now, the Sun is about ten times larger than the planet Jupiter, and 100 times larger than the planet Earth. When it becomes a red giant, it will be 200 times larger than it is now – although it will actually lose mass as it grows, so it won't be as heavy, and won't exert as large a gravitational pull on the planets.

So will all the planets just fly off into Space?
Some might. But everything from Mars inwards (including us) will probably be swallowed and frazzled by the Sun as it grows.

STARS FORM IN A NEBULA, FROM COLLAPSING CLOUDS OF INTERSTELLA GAS AND DUST...	THE STAR BURNS HAPPILY THROUGHOUT ITS LIFE...	UNTIL, AT THE END, IT BEGINS TO EXPAND INTO A RED GIANT...
ONCE ALL THE GASES HAVE BURNED AWAY...	ALL THAT'S LEFT IS WHAT'S KNOWN AS A WHITE DWARF	AS THIS COOLS, THE STAR THEN BECOMES A BLACK DWARF
	O	•

That doesn't sound too good! So what happens after that?

After that, the Sun will burn away as a red giant for a while longer, with the core still shrinking and compressing, and the outer layers still expanding. Once all the helium atoms in the core have fused into carbon atoms, it will stop shrinking, become stable and release most of its energy. The outer layers will then drift off into Space, forming a shell-like gas cloud (confusingly called a planetary nebula), and only the small, white-hot core will remain in the centre. With this, the Sun will have become an unreactive **white**

dwarf star. Over time, this will steadily lose heat and become a lifeless black dwarf.

Not THAT – I mean, what happens after the Sun becomes a red giant and swallows the Earth? Who *cares* what happens after *that* if we're all frazzled!

Oh. *That.*

Well, if the human race is still around, hopefully we'll have hopped the planet (and possibly the solar system) by then, and made our home somewhere else in Space (more about Space colonies in Chapter 6). But, all in all, it could be worse.

Worse? What could be worse than your Sun swelling up and frazzling you?

Well, as I said before, there are a few ways a star can end its life – some more dramatic and destructive than others. Thankfully our Sun isn't massive enough for the worst of these to happen . . .

GET IT SORTED – MASS VS DENSITY

In the last section, we learned the difference between weight and mass. Now we're talking about enormous stars that **grow and shrink** as they **lose and gain mass.** It can all get very confusing if you don't understand what **density** is. So here goes.

Density is a measure of **how much mass fits into a given volume** (shape and size) of object.

So if two objects with the **same mass** are **different sizes** – say, a beach ball and an apple – then the **larger** object (the beach ball) has **less density**. On the flipside, the **smaller** object (the apple) has **more density**. Get it?

Now as a star ages the stuff it's made of (its **mass**) is converted into energy, in the form of **heat, light and radiation** – a bit like the way a wooden log loses mass as it is burned to produce heat and light in a campfire. But, unlike the log, the star **doesn't shrink in size as it loses mass** – at least not at first. Instead, it swells, becoming **less dense** (like an enormous beach ball). Then later on, it **contracts** and becomes **more dense** (like a huge, super-hard apple) before ending its life as a dwarf star.

Now try to keep the idea of beach balls, apples and density in mind as we go on.

What happens when a star burns out?

It depends how big they are. The smallest ones just fizzle out, while more massive ones may swell and explode before doing the same. The most massive stars may explode and then collapse in on themselves, creating a mysterious and sinister black hole.

Why does the size matter so much?

The remaining mass of the star at the end of its life is what determines whether it will implode, explode or simply fizzle out.

As we've already seen, the fate of your average dwarf star is typically a long, slow **burnout**. Red dwarfs burn for trillions of years before collapsing into white dwarfs. Sun-like yellow dwarfs, however, swell up, burn off their outer layers to form a planetary nebula and end up in the same state within 10 billion years or so.

Stars much larger than our Sun, though, really do 'live fast and die young', as they burn through their nuclear fuel that much quicker. And a different fate awaits them at the end of their lives.

Stars that start out over ten times more massive than the Sun expand to become not just red giants, but **red supergiants**. These monsters are the largest stars in the Universe – most being 1,000–1,500 times larger than the Sun, yet usually much cooler at just 3,000–4,000K.

Yikes. That's pretty big. So what happens after that?

One of a few things. The star only remains as a red supergiant* for a few hundred thousand to a few million years. If the nuclear reactions inside it slow down for any reason, it may shrink to become a slightly smaller (but much hotter and brighter) **blue supergiant**.** Some stars even swing backwards and forwards between these two states for millions of years. But eventually the end must come. And, when it does, these big boys do it in style.

Once most of the hydrogen in the supergiant's core is used up, the core collapses in on itself, creating enormous pressures and temperatures. This kick-starts new nuclear fusion reactions, and forges heavier and heavier elements inside the core, like carbon, silicon, magnesium and iron. In fact, all the heavy elements found on the Earth and other planets are forged in dying stars like this – including the stuff we're made of. Which is pretty crazy, when you think about it. It means we're all made of star-stuff!

Whoa. That is pretty freaky. So *then* what?

Then the core keeps burning for a while longer, until the pressure drops and it collapses again. This happens over and over until finally the core becomes so

---

* Betelgeuse, which we found within the constellation of Orion in Chapter 3, is an example of a red supergiant star.

** Rigel, also found within Orion, is a well-known blue supergiant.

heavy that it literally can't support its own weight. It implodes catastrophically, like a massive building collapsing in on itself, creating unimaginable amounts of heat, pressure and energy. The rebounding flash and explosion is more powerful than *trillions* upon *trillions* of our most powerful nuclear warheads. In a supernova, a dying supergiant star will release more energy in a week than our Sun does in its entire lifetime. And in one spectacular blowout, the supergiant star is no more.

So what's left behind?

That depends on how much unexploded 'stuff' is left behind – as the final form that a 'dying' star takes depends on **how much mass remains** after the supernova takes place.

If the remaining material has 1.5 to 3 times as much mass as our Sun, it'll collapse to form a supersmall, super-dense **neutron star**. These measure just 10 miles (14 km) across (about the size of London or New York City) but are so heavy that a teaspoonful of neutron star material would weigh roughly 10 million tonnes – or the same as roughly 15,000 jumbo jets!

If the remaining material has three Suns' worth of mass or more, the core may collapse to form a **black hole** – a supermassive object with so much gravitational pull that within a certain distance around it nothing can escape. Not even light – which is what makes the black hole invisible.

A SUPERMASSIVE STAR CAN BE TEN TIMES BIGGER THAN OUR OWN SUN AND WHEN IT BEGINS TO DIE IT BECOMES A RED SUPERGIANT...	EVENTUALLY, THE RED SUPERGIANT COLLAPSES IN ON ITSELF. THIS IS CALLED A SUPERNOVA...	IT CAN KEEP COLLAPSING IN ON ITSELF, FORMING A BLACK HOLE, WHICH WILL SUCK IN EVERYTHING IN ITS PATH...
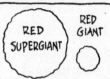		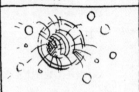

Does that happen much? I mean, are there lots of black holes around?

Stars massive enough to form them are very rare, but there are still more black holes than you'd think. In fact, astronomers now believe there may be a black hole at the centre of every galaxy in the Universe – including ours.

What? But if that were true, wouldn't it suck us in and eat us?

Not at all. Contrary to popular belief, black holes don't just suck in surrounding stars and planets like giant Space Hoovers. Although their gravitational pull is incredibly strong close up, beyond a certain point, the black hole becomes less dangerous as the gravitational pull is less powerful.

As we've already seen, the Sun – as a yellow dwarf star – is just not big enough to turn into a black hole. But if it suddenly did it wouldn't suck in all the planets and eat them. It would actually have little effect on the planets' orbits at all – they would simply keep circling their black hole sun as before.

Of course, all the lights would go out, too, so the planets would soon freeze and everything on them would die . . .

Yikes!

. . . but that's another issue. The point is that beyond a certain distance, the black hole doesn't suck in or destroy anything at all. We call this boundary the **event horizon** of the black hole. This forms an invisible sphere around the **very centre** of the black hole, which in turn is known as the **singularity** (or very centre of the hole) itself.

The distance of the event horizon from the centre is called the **Schwarzschild radius**, and it differs depending on the mass of the black hole itself. It might seem strange to think that a **hole** can have mass, but, in fact, black holes are not just massive, many are **supermassive**. Want to know what that means? Then read on . . .

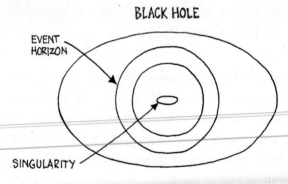

BLACK HOLE

EVENT HORIZON

SINGULARITY

How big can a black hole get?

While the 'hole' in Space itself is tinier than an atom, the surrounding sphere of inescapable blackness can extend anywhere from a few millimetres to trillions of kilometres across.

I don't get it. How can a planet-swallowing hole be tinier than an atom?

Well, the singularity (or hole) itself is literally no size at all – it's a whole star's worth of mass crushed up into a single point of **infinite density** and **zero volume**. But, if you're talking about the size of the 'hole' into which things fall (and never come out), then that means the distance from one edge of the event horizon to the other. And, looking at them this way, there's actually quite a wide range.

From 'edge to edge', most black holes are fairly small. A typical **stellar mass black hole** will measure less than 40 miles (60 km) across – less than half the size of Belgium – yet it contains the same mass as one to ten average-sized dwarf stars or suns.

Intermediate black holes contain thousands of times more mass than our Sun, but measure just a few thousand kilometres across – about the same size as the Earth.

The largest, called **supermassive black holes**, contain **hundreds of billions** of times as much mass as our Sun, and have a Schwartzchild Radius of up to 1.5 trillion km (1 trillion miles). That's roughly the same distance from the Earth to the Sun. So if our Sun magically turned into one of these monsters, the Earth would be sitting right at the edge of the event horizon, a thin sliver of Space away from being sucked in and lost forever.

Although no one has ever detected one, it's also possible that **micro black holes** once existed in the early Universe, and may still exist to this day. These would have a mass similar to that of the Moon, but would measure less than half a millimetre across. Some physicists think it may even be possible to create micro black holes like this in laboratories, by smashing sub-atomic particles together at immense speeds with a particle accelerator*.

Whoa! Hang on a minute – that sounds a bit dangerous!

Don't worry – it hasn't happened yet. And even if it does, physicists say that the micro-hole would only live for a fraction of a second before decaying and disappearing, and the microscopic amount of energy they produced wouldn't be enough to power a light-bulb, let alone destroy the planet.

---

* Like the Large Hadron Collider (LHC) at the European Centre for Nuclear Research (CERN). That one accelerates particles through a huge magnet-lined tube 16 miles (27 km) in circumference, buried 330 feet (100 m) underground near Geneva, Switzerland.

But what if they made a supermassive one?
They can't, as that would require a super-amount of mass – more mass than is found in the entire solar system. So relax – the end of the world isn't coming. Or at least if it does it won't be via a black hole.

Whew! That's a relief.
Astronomers *do* think, however, that there *is* a super-massive black hole lurking at the centre of our galaxy . . .

What?!? Why do they think that?
Because for many years they've been pointing their telescopes and instruments at other galaxies and detecting huge amounts of energy – coming from an invisible source somewhere in the centre. One explanation for this is that there's a supermassive black hole in the centre of each galaxy, with many, many stars orbiting tightly around it.

As these densely packed stars collide with each other and lose mass and momentum, they may fall out of orbit and drift inside the event horizon. The black hole then devours these stars, never to be seen again.

But if they're never seen again, how do we know the stars or the black hole are there at all?
Because before they go the colliding stars at the very *edge* of the black hole may reach temperatures of millions of degrees, and release massive amounts of

energy in the form of x-rays, gamma rays and other forms of radiation. It's this energy that the astronomers are detecting, and this is what gives away the invisible black hole's position in Space.

Although we haven't detected energy bursts like this in the centre of our own galaxy, looking at the orbits of the densely packed stars there has revealed that there pretty much *must* be an invisible object keeping them in orbit. And only a supermassive black hole could be large enough to do it, yet remain unseen by telescopes.

So what would happen if you were flying a spaceship right near a black hole, and you went for a Space walk, and you . . . you know . . . accidentally fell in?

Well, we're not really sure, since we've never been anywhere near one and, even if we had, no one (or no *thing*) could ever come out of a black hole to tell the tale. But from what we know about black-hole physics, it probably wouldn't be good.

What do you mean?

Well, once past the event horizon, the gravitational forces within the black hole become so strong that they would rip you apart. If you fell in feet-first, the pull on your feet would be thousands of times stronger than the pull on your head, so it would stretch you and snap you like an elastic band.

Ouch! What about if you fell in headfirst? Wait – don't answer that. I can imagine. At least it might be a quicker way to go, I suppose . . .

Not necessarily. Thanks to the strange physics of the black hole as a supermassive, infinitely dense object, it may warp space-time around you so that it seems to take forever to fall in. And all the while you're being stretched, snapped and roasted by the radiation from the stars colliding nearby.

Oooooh – that's gotta hurt. But what about the idea of flying through a black hole and coming out somewhere else in the Universe?

Well, some physicists think it might be possible, but since nothing ever comes out of a black hole once it goes in, we have no way of testing that idea. It's possible that – if you could somehow survive the journey through the singularity – you might emerge at another singularity at some distant point in Space, or in another dimension, or even in a parallel universe. But even if it were true that two black holes could form 'stargates' like this, and you managed to enter one, you'd still have the problem of exiting the gate at the 'other side' – which would, after all, be another (seemingly inescapable) black hole.

All things considered, I wouldn't want to try it.

Me neither. Okay – so what is that massive black hole *doing* in the middle of our galaxy?

Not much, these days. It just kind of sits there, being dense.

Like the people on those reality TV programmes?
Errr . . . kind of. But black holes do a little more than that. In fact, most astronomers now believe that black holes may actually help *build* galaxies in the first place. Although they have little effect on (all but the very closest) stars in a fully formed galaxy, it seems that their sheer mass helps to assemble the stars into newly forming ones.

Is that why stars form galaxies? Because a black hole draws them in around it?
Not quite. Some astronomers used to think maybe that's what happens, but we now know that a black hole doesn't really affect anything much beyond its event horizon. So while it could draw stars into orbit with its mass – much as other stars do when they or- bit each other – it couldn't possibly affect the orbits of stars thousands of light years away, at the outer edge of the galaxy.

But the size of (or total number of stars within) a galaxy appears related to the size of the black hole in the middle. So this suggests that the galaxy and black hole form at the same time, from the same material, and this influences the galaxy's final shape and size.

Which brings us neatly to our next question . . .

Why are galaxies shaped like spirals?

Not all of them are. Spirals are just one of several shapes a galaxy may develop into. Others form flat discs like sombrero hats, ovoid balls like squashed eggs or irregular blobs with no real defined shape. It all depends on how the galaxy is structured and built.

Whoa!

Yep. And even the spiral ones have different shapes and numbers of spiral arms. From piecing together snapshots of galaxies of different ages, astronomers have learned that specific patterns of star formation, development and gravitational attraction can make galaxies of many different shapes and sizes. To help us study galaxy structures, good old **Edwin Hubble** came up with the first classification system for them based on the most common shapes that he saw:

- **Spiral galaxies** contain millions or billions of stars rotating in a wide, flat disc around a central point, where a supermassive black hole probably lurks unseen. A bright spherical cloud of young **yellow dwarf** stars circles tightly around the centre.

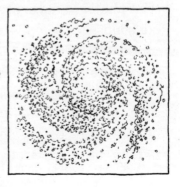

Within the disc, the stars are arranged into two or more curving lines – called the spiral arms[*] – whirling outward from the centre.

- In **barred spiral** galaxies, the arms seem to trail from a long, straight bar which runs through the centre (or **nucleus**) of the galaxy – a bit like pendants streaming from the blades of a windmill. These straight bars form as the orbits of adjacent stars align  with each other due to gravity. About 80 per cent of all spiral galaxies are barred spirals like these, so that must happen pretty often!

- **Elliptical galaxies** have no arms at all, and look like ovals or ellipses when viewed on a flat photograph (so presumably look like eggs or squashed footballs in three dimensions). Although most of the galaxies we've listed on star maps are spirals, astronomers think that most galaxies in the Universe are really elliptical. This

---

[*] In reality, there are probably millions of stars in the dark spaces *between* the arms. What we're really seeing is just the brightest (blue supergiant) stars forming at the leading edges of each arm, while dimming or dying stars trail along behind.

is because they tend to be smaller (and therefore dimmer) than spiral galaxies, so are much more difficult to see.

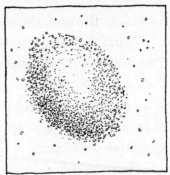

Over three-quarters of all known galaxies are spirals, barred spirals and ellipticals. But there are two other less common classes.

- **Lenticular** (or lens-shaped) **galaxies** look like spiral galaxies without the spirals. The stars within them are spread fairly evenly across a wide, flat disc, making it look a bit like a CD with a glowing marble stuck in the middle.

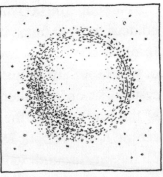

- **Irregular galaxies** come in a variety of random shapes, and include all those that don't fit into the other classes (spiral, barred spiral, elliptical and lenticular).

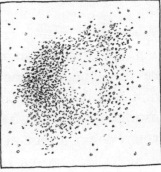

Galaxies also come in a wide range of **sizes**.

Dwarf spiral galaxies contain millions of stars similar to our Sun, while larger spiral galaxies may contain *billions* of stars. **Lenticular** and **irregular galaxies** tend to contain less than a quarter as many stars as the average **spiral galaxy**, while **elliptical galaxies** are usually smaller still, with less than one millionth as many stars as our own spiral galaxy, the Milky Way.

So ours is a spiral one, then?
Yep. An average-sized spiral galaxy with a disc of stars about 100,000 light years across, circling a galactic nuclear bulge about 30,000 light years wide. In all, it contains between **200 to 400 billion** stars, of which our Sun is just one. The Sun, and our solar system, sit on an outer spiral arm about two-thirds of the way towards the edge of the galaxy from the centre. It takes about 250 million years for it to circle all the way around. So it has only managed to do one lap since the time of the dinosaurs!

Whoa. That's pretty crazy.
Yep. Kind of blows your mind to think about it. And get this – the next time you look up at the night sky and spot the bright band of stars across it (which astronomers call the Milky Way), think about what you're doing. Although you may not realize it, you're actually looking out along the disc of the galaxy

(either towards the centre, or towards the edge). Look anywhere else in the sky, and your eyes are leaving the galaxy and heading out into the wider Universe.

Whoa! Now that's pretty cool. So how many galaxies are there?

We don't know for sure. But astronomers estimate that there are over **100 billion** galaxies in the known Universe, most of them arranged in clusters with wide tracts of near-empty Space in between. We also know that galaxies collide, merge and eat each other – so, many that start out as spirals may form disordered blobs and clusters as they crash and fuse into others.

Do they all have planets?

Almost certainly.

Really? Can we see them?

Sadly, no – because other galaxies are so far away that we can't yet hope to see details of planets and moons within the stars there. Even the closest one – the **Canis Major** dwarf galaxy – is 25,000 light years away. So we learn most of what we know about other solar systems by observing our own, and assuming others are built in similar ways.

Not all stars may have the right conditions for life, however. And some astronomers argue that complex life on Earth may be a unique freak of the Universe. But we know there are millions of solar systems and billions of planets and moons within our own galaxy (more on these **exoplanets** later). And we expect a good number of these to be capable of supporting life. Maybe not exactly like our own – but life of some kind.

So, looking at the numbers and odds, it seems highly unlikely that we're the only solar system with life in our galaxy, and *extremely* unlikely that life exists *nowhere* else amongst the trillions of other systems in the billions of galaxies spread throughout the Universe.

And even though a great deal about other galaxies and solar systems remains unknown, we've discovered a *lot* about our own solar system (which we'll be exploring in the next chapter). And we now – at least – know what kinds of things to expect when we look elsewhere.

Now it's time to set off – on a whizzing whirlwind tour of our own special place in Space . . .

Stars and galaxies word search

Black hole
Event horizon
Nebular
Spiral

Blue giant
Hubble
Protostar
Supermassive

Elliptical
Lenticular
Red dwarf
Supernova

```
Y Q S U K J T T N G R H H X W C J J L S
Y C L Y N T A R E D D W A R F K D R Z U
O M M P Z N X G H R S J R E A P J E U P
U V F R N A C O T O V J Q B T X L H X E
N W M O N I N Y R C U F L V C B P J H R
N W Q T S G N U U L D U V X B V J P H N
D Y E O A E P E Q X Q H G U H G O S R O
G S K S I U V T U F B L H H L O D Q W V
L U Q T R L Q E L Y F I K L Y G P J R A
C P X A H B L E N T I C U L A R C N T O
A E F R Y C V I T T T U E V P S L N V U
R R H O O I U E F R H L H U S A R Z C R
A M S N L N H R O P O O K C C P K W V U
L A S E W U U Z K H H W R I K P N O K I
U S P C A G H A K F L O T I Z X O K S M
B S I V I X O C F V Y P S R Z N F D E O
E I R E T G A Q D Q I R S Q K O F A Y Z
N V A H Y L V S A L V T Y Q A V N M B C
R E L V B T H X L G Y M T H T J I F B S
A E V X R I O E T L N U Q Q E O E D E A
```

(answers on page 252)

5.
A Trip Around the Solar System

Cool! So where do we start?
On Earth, of course! We'll begin with a quick intro to the system and a quick whizz around the **Earth-Moon system**. Then after that it's up to you.

You can head towards the centre of the solar system, passing **Venus** and **Mercury** on your way to the **Sun**. Or you can head outwards, stopping briefly on **Mars** before tearing through the **asteroid belt** and onwards to **Jupiter, Saturn, Uranus, Neptune** and beyond. Along the way we'll also explore dwarf planets, moons, comets and more.

Brilliant! When do we leave?
Right away. The ship is on the launch pad, fully fuelled and ready to go. Just a quick pre-flight briefing, and you're ready for blast-off . . .

Pre-flight briefing: know your solar system

While you're strapping in and suiting up, let's have a quick run-through of where you're headed.

Our solar system is roughly 4.5 billion years old, and consists of a central yellow dwarf star called

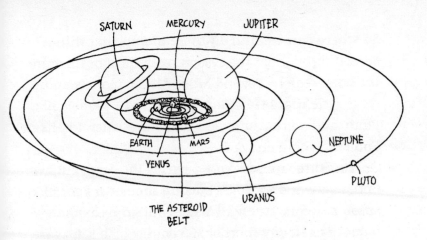

Labels: SATURN, MERCURY, JUPITER, EARTH, MARS, NEPTUNE, VENUS, PLUTO, THE ASTEROID BELT, URANUS

Sol (better known as the Sun) surrounded by eight planets, two asteroid belts, several dwarf planets, a huge shell of icy comets and over 170 moons!

A *hundred and seventy* moons? Wow!

Yep. If you had a fast enough spaceship, you could visit a different one every year for your summer holiday, and still never get through half of them in a whole lifetime.

And what's a dwarf planet?

It's a large, rounded object that is much bigger than an asteroid or comet, but not quite big enough to qualify as a planet. Unlike moons, dwarf planets orbit the Sun directly, rather than orbiting other planets. There are at least five of them in our solar system, the most well-known being Pluto. But there are probably at least forty or fifty more. We'll learn more about dwarf planets later.

So where can we find all these moons and things?
Spread throughout the system, with most of them in the outer regions beyond Mars. All the planets in the solar system orbit the Sun, as do dwarf planets like Pluto and Ceres, and non-planetary asteroids like Eris.

The Earth, as you know, circles the Sun roughly once every 364.75 days, making the Earth year just short of 365 days long. (Actually, it's approximately a quarter of a day short of 365 days, which is why we have 'leap years'. We add an extra day to February every four years in order to keep the cycle even. Without this, our calendars would soon be out of whack.)

The other planets and objects, however, orbit at different distances from the Sun, tracing out elliptical paths that are shorter (for those closer to the Sun) or longer (for those further away) than that of the Earth. This means that a Martian year is longer than an Earth year, but a Venusian year is much shorter.

When we get to each of the planets in turn, we'll look at how long each one takes to orbit the Sun, and therefore how long its years and seasons are. After all, it's cold enough on Mars already, so you don't really want to land there in winter!

Yeah, s'pose not.
So, are you ready to go?

Almost. One more thing: how did we figure all this stuff out? Like, how long a Martian year is, and how cold it is in winter?

Well, as we saw in Chapter 2, Johannes Kepler figured out that the path and speed of a planet's orbit depends upon how far away it is from the Sun, and Isaac Newton later worked out that this, in turn, depends on how big the planet is. That's why the four small planets known as the **Terrestrial planets (Mercury, Venus, Earth and Mars)** orbit close to the Sun, while the more massive **Jovian planets (Jupiter, Saturn, Uranus and Neptune)** orbit at much greater distances.

Okay, but why do the planets bother orbiting the Sun at all? Did the Sun pluck them from outer Space with its gravity?

Good guess, but not quite. The Sun's gravity is what *holds* the planets and other objects in orbit. But we're pretty sure that it didn't capture them as they whizzed by. Astronomers think that the Sun, the planets and most of the asteroids, comets and moons that make up the solar system all formed at the same time, from the same cloud of rotation dust and gas.

Groan! Not the gas clouds again. Is *everything* in the Universe made of gas and dust?

Pretty much, yes. Or at least most things started out that way, soon after the Big Bang – more about that in Chapter 6. But the point is that the bits of the solar system all spin around the Sun because they *started out* as part of the *same* spinning gas cloud.

Over 4.5 billion years ago, a huge dust cloud in our region of the galaxy started to condense and flatten out, turning into a huge spinning disc. As the cloud contracted further, momentum caused its spin to increase, like an ice-skater pulling in their arms during a pirouette. Soon, the centre of the spinning cloud collapsed to form a protostar (that would soon become our Sun), with a massive disc of dust, gas and ice packed in tightly around it. Within a few tens of millions of years, planets began forming within this disc as bits of it clotted together under their own gravity. Soon, they would be fully formed and more or less the same shape and size as they are now.

So that was it, all done?
Not quite. Back then, the planets were all more tightly packed around the Sun, with a massive cloud of rocky, icy asteroids sitting around the outside. Then about 3.9 billion years ago, something pretty dramatic happened that rearranged the outer bits of the system.

What was that?
Basically, the system's most massive planets, Jupiter and Saturn, started to synchronize their orbits around the Sun. Then their combined gravity pulled Uranus

and Neptune out of their previous orbits and flung them outwards into the giant asteroid cloud. The two planets smashed through the asteroids like a pair of bowling balls, scattering rocks and ice everywhere, and sending thousands of asteroids and comets back towards the inner planets. For the next 100 million years, these asteroids and comets smashed into Mars, Earth, Venus and Mercury, altering their atmospheres and orbits, and possibly even kick-starting the first life on Earth. They also bombarded the Moon, creating many of the craters we can still see on its surface – evidence of a 4-billion-year-old cosmic bowling game that changed the solar system forever.

Cool! Okay – I'm ready now. Let's go.
Roger that. Countdown commencing.
  First stop: Earth orbit.

3 . . . 2 . . . 1 . . . lift-off!

The Earth–Moon system

There's no place like home.

What makes the Earth so special?

Oooh, lots of things. It has water in all three forms – solid ice, liquid water and gaseous vapour. It has a magnetic field and ozone layer that shields its surface from harmful radiation. It has the perfect range of temperature, pressure and other atmospheric conditions for the evolution of life. All in all, it's not a bad place to be, actually!

For obvious reasons, we know more about the Earth and Moon than any other part of the solar system. After all – these are the only two bits of it we've ever actually set foot on.

The Earth is a rocky ball around 8,000 miles (12,700 km) wide at the equator. It spins on a central axis that runs through the north and south poles, tilted at a heady 23 degrees from vertical. It rotates once every twenty-four hours, and its spin causes it to bulge around the middle, so it's almost – but not quite – a perfect sphere. It is the largest of the **Terrestrial** (or 'earthly') **planets** – the four, dense, rocky planets that sit closest to the Sun.

The Earth's continents and oceans sit atop a rocky crust about 60 miles (100 km) thick, which in turn floats above a semi-solid mantle of molten rock 1,800 miles (3,000 km) deep. Beneath that lies a liquid metal outer core, and a solid metal inner core – both made mostly of iron and nickel.

It has a breathable atmosphere
of about 77 per cent nitrogen,
21 per cent oxygen, and 2 per
cent other gases. Amongst
these, water vapour cycles life-
giving water between the seas
and land, while carbon dioxide
and other 'greenhouse' gases help
reflect heat back towards the Earth, keeping it
much warmer than it would otherwise be. Surface
temperatures range from -90°C (-130°F) at the icy
poles to 60°C (140°F) in the deserts, but the average is
a toasty, comfortable 15°C (60°F).

**Doesn't that change with the seasons too? Why
does that happen?**
The seasons change as the Earth moves through its
year-long orbit around the Sun, exposing the northern and southern halves (or hemispheres) of the
planet to more or less sunlight at different points of
the orbit. This is not – as some people think – because
the Earth is closer or further from the Sun at these
times. It's because the Earth's axis is always tilted the
same way, and doesn't rotate as the Earth spins and
orbits the Sun*.

---

* Well, it does. But it takes about 26,000 years, so most of us don't
notice the effect.

During summer in the northern hemisphere, the top of the axis (or north pole) leans towards the Sun, leaving the northern half of the planet in direct sunlight (and heating the land, air and seas) for longer. This gives long summer days and a hot summer season. The southern hemisphere, meanwhile, spends longer in the shade at this time of year, giving longer nights, shorter days and less time for the land, air and seas to heat up. Hence, short wintry days, and a cold winter season. It's a bit like tilting the sticks on a rotating doner kebab – one side gets 'grilled' longer than the other.

Six months later, the Earth has moved to the other side of the Sun, and the north pole is tilted away from the Sun. Now the situation is reversed – the northern hemisphere gets less sunlight, casting it into winter, while the southern hemisphere enjoys more sunlight and its long-awaited summer.

What about spring and autumn?
Spring and autumn are simply the bits in between these two extremes, when sunlight strikes the Earth side-on, and the northern and southern hemispheres receive more or less equal amounts of heating. In spring, the atmosphere gradually heats up as the days get longer, while in autumn, the atmosphere gradually cools as the days get shorter. Simple.

It's this ideal pattern of heating and cooling, together with its precise distance from the Sun, which makes the Earth so special, and such a superbly unique place for supporting life in the solar system.

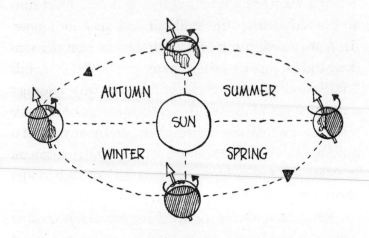

Why is the distance so important?
Well, at the birth of the solar system, the distance from the Sun at which each planet settled into orbit ultimately decided how hot it would be. This, in turn, affects the nature of its atmosphere, oceans (if any) and weather systems.

The planets closest to the Sun have no water, as they are so hot that all of their oceans have boiled off. Those further away than the Earth – if they have any water at all – only have it in the form of solid, frozen ice. The Earth is at the right distance from the Sun, and therefore the right temperature, to keep water in all three forms. So it has solid ice at the poles and on mountain tops. It has liquid water in its oceans, lakes and rivers. And it has gaseous water vapour in its atmosphere (which condenses into liquid droplets in clouds, and falls to earth as rain or snow).

So the only thing that makes Earth special is how far from the Sun it is? So, if Mars was a bit closer, it would be just like the Earth?
That's most of it, yes. But it's also to do with how big and dense the planet is. This is because the gases that remain in a planet's atmosphere are held there by gravity. If the gas is too light (or the planet so small that it doesn't have enough gravitational attraction), then parts of its atmosphere 'leak' into Space.

This is why Venus, as we'll see later, has such a hellish atmosphere – the lighter gases slowly leaked away from it, leaving only heavier (and toxic) carbon dioxide and sulphur dioxide gas behind[*].

The Earth also has a strong magnetic field, generated by the movement of its metal core, which helps protect it from dangerous solar and cosmic radiation. So there are many reasons why the Earth is such a great place to live.

What about the Moon? We've been there, haven't we? Could we live there too?
Well, let's head up there and find out . . .

---

* In fact, this is even happening to the Earth. We're leaking hydrogen into Space too – just a great deal slower than Venus has been. Eventually this will dry up entire oceans and drastically affect weather patterns. But it'll take a few billion years, so nothing to worry about just yet!

Walking on the Moon

So what's it really like on the Moon?

According to the twelve astronauts who have had the rare privilege to walk on it, the Moon's surface is like a desert – bleak, yet beautiful. It has rocks, boulders, mountains and craters formed by past meteorite impacts. It also has wide, flat plains called **maria** (from the ancient Latin word meaning 'seas'). Each plain (or **mare**), it seems, was formed by volcanic lava flows bubbling up from underneath, which spread out to make a smooth, flat surface.

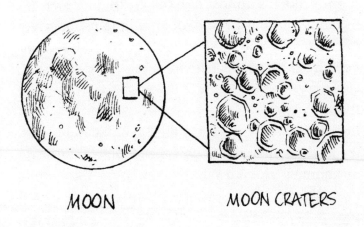

MOON   MOON CRATERS

There are volcanoes up there?

There are no active volcanoes on the Moon any more, but at one time there were many. Just like the Earth, the Moon has layers. At the surface is a rocky crust about the same thickness as the Earth's. Beneath that, it has a semi-liquid mantle surrounding an inner and outer core. For 100–150 million years after the Moon was formed, the churning mantle was spewing molten rock up through holes in the Moon's crust, breaching the surface as lava and creating many volcanoes. But the Moon's volcanoes have long been extinct, as the Moon's interior quickly cooled and stabilized. And the few that now remain are small domes just a few hundred metres high.

Wow. I thought the Moon was just a big rock. With all those mountains, seas and volcanoes, it sounds like it's almost like the Earth.
In many ways, it is. And, according to astronomers, there's a very good reason for that. The Moon *came from* the Earth in the first place.

It did?
It seems so. You've heard of the Big Bang, right? Well, the leading theory as to how the Moon was formed is nicknamed 'The Big Whack'. And it goes something like this . . .

The Big Whack
Around 4.5 billion years ago, when the Earth and solar system were still young, the Earth was just one of several planet-sized objects that were growing and whipping around in the dusty primordial disc surrounding the Sun. Well, one of these objects – a massive asteroid of

a dwarf planet, perhaps – whacked into the Earth and smashed a huge chunk out of it. The resulting debris flew into Space as billions of tonnes of dust and molten rock. This debris was then drawn into a ring around the Earth (much like Saturn's, only those are made of ice, and remain that way – more on that when we get there later on), and eventually clotted together by gravity to form a solid lump.

| ASTEROID/PLANETOID COLLIDES WITH THE EARTH... | DEBRIS FORMS A RING AROUND THE EARTH... | WHICH SLOWY BECOMES THE MOON |

For a while this new satellite (or moon) stayed molten, and the surface was a fiery place filled with volcanic eruptions and lava flows. Then it started to cool, and after about 900 million years it reached a state which remained more or less unchanged to this day. A cold, crusty ball just over a quarter of the size of the Earth, which circles our planet once every 27.3 days, at an average distance of 240,000 miles (384,400 km).

Is there no air, water or gravity on the Moon, then?

Lacking the size (and therefore the gravity) to keep them there, the Moon has no water, no air and no atmosphere. This also means it has nothing to absorb and hold radiation from the Sun, so surface temperatures range from an ultra-freezing -170°C in the shade to a roasting 130°C in direct sunlight.

The Moon does, however, have gravity. In fact, every object in the Universe does – with a strength that simply depends on how big it is. But, being much smaller than the Earth, it simply generates much less of a pull. At the surface, its gravitational pull is around one-sixth of that of the Earth – which is why the astronauts on those old Moon-landing video clips seemed to bounce around as if they were on wires.

Yeah, but I read something on the internet that said they *were* on wires. That NASA faked the whole thing.

Sadly, there are some ill-informed people out there who actually believe this. And they even think that there's 'proof' of this 'moon-landing conspiracy', in the details of pictures, video clips and reports of how it was done.

Did we really land on the Moon, or did NASA just fake it?

Quite simply – no. There was no conspiracy, and all the 'proof' the internet nutters put forward is easily explained away if you know anything about physics. Here are the top three, for starters:

1) **In the moon-landing pictures, you can't see any stars in the background. That's because they weren't taken on the Moon – they were taken in a film studio somewhere.**
   Brilliant. Until you realize that the Moon's surface and the astronauts' suits were reflecting very bright sunlight. So to prevent them from overexposing the film (and making the whole picture come out white), they had to snap the camera shutters open and closed very quickly. This didn't give enough time for the much fainter light from the stars to appear in the picture. NEXT.

2) **The cameras and video cameras wouldn't have worked on the Moon, because it's 130°C in the sun, and -170°C in the shade. Even if they survived the heat undamaged, the lenses would steam up every time they turned around.**
   Believe it or not, the cameras were actually *designed* for use on the Moon. They were covered

in a reflective material which kept them mostly unaffected by sunlight. And to 'steam up', a lens requires water vapour to condense out of the air, to form water droplets on a surface (otherwise known as condensation). On the Moon, there is neither air nor water. NEXT.

3) **The radiation (or Van Allen) belt held around the Earth by its magnetic field would have killed the astronauts before they even got to the Moon.**

Bzzzzt! Wrong again. The radiation in the Van Allen belt *could* kill you . . . if you stayed within it for *several weeks*, soaking it up. But the Apollo astronauts only stayed there for about an hour – long enough to pass through it, and no more. Plus the Apollo ships were shielded for radiation, just in case. NEXT . . .

. . . and so the list goes on.

For all the so-called 'proof' these conspiracy theories put forward, every bit of it turns out to be false or misguided. So you can file these fake Moon-landing theories under 'nutter', along with modern sightings of Elvis and real-life alien abductions.

Landing on the Moon was one of the greatest achievements in the history of humankind. One day, we may go back to explore it further, or even to mine or live on the Moon's surface (more about that in Chapter 6). So it's a little sad that some people want to mock this wonderful achievement with silly, sneering suspicions. Besides that, there are plenty of interesting (and real) things to find out about the Moon, so why bother mucking about with daft conspiracy theories?

Why does the Moon change shape?
It's to do with how light from the Sun is reflected off it. Depending on the relative positions of the Earth, Moon and Sun, different parts of the Moon become lit and shadowed. The lit-up parts make the Moon shapes we're so familiar with. Sometimes, of course, the Moon gets right between the Earth and Sun. Then things really get interesting . . .

Hold on – I'm not seeing this. I lost you at 'relative positions'.
Okay, so you've noticed that the Moon seems to change shape from week to week – or, if you're looking carefully, from day to day. Right?

Right. Sometimes it's a full circle. And sometimes it's a half-circle or a crescent. Sometimes the left half is lit up, and sometimes the right. And sometimes it even disappears altogether.
You're right, it does. When it vanishes like that, we call it a new moon.

So what's with that? If the Moon's just like a big mirror that circles around us and reflects sunlight, then shouldn't it always be there? I mean, it's not like the Sun can *go out*. So the Moon can't just *disappear*.

You're right. The Sun is always there, shining away. And the Moon can't disappear.

But it can *move*. Which means it can also *hide* sometimes.

Eh? What do you mean by that?

Well, we know the Moon circles the Earth every 27.3 days, completing each lap in just under a month. That's much slower than the twenty-four hours the Earth takes to spin on its axis, which is why the Moon (when it's visible) rises and sets, just like the Sun.

But if you think about it, in order for the Moon to *always* be visible, it would have to maintain the same angle to the Sun and Earth year round. So to keep a position behind the Earth at 180 degrees from the Sun (as it does at full moon), it would have to orbit *halfway around the Earth* in the same time it took the Earth to travel *halfway around the Sun*. That would mean the Moon would be orbiting us once a year, rather than once a month.

Instead, the Moon laps the Earth twelve times faster than we lap the Sun, like an excited puppy running rings around us as we take our slow annual stroll. Because of this, the Moon's angle to the Earth

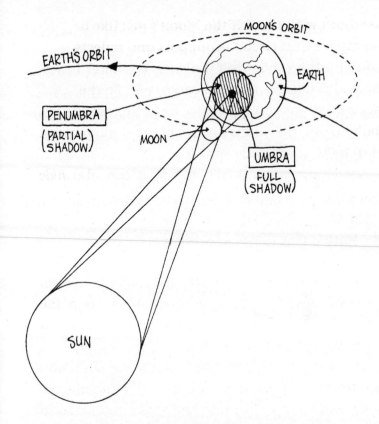

is constantly changing. So sometimes it's behind the Earth, sometimes it's between the Earth and the Sun, and most of the time it's off to one side.

Remember also that the Moon isn't a flat mirror – it's more like a *mirrorball*. So it only reflects light from the side illuminated by the Sun, and most of the time only part of this lit-up side will be visible to us on Earth. This combination of movement and partial reflection is what causes the changing shapes of the Moon, otherwise known as **lunar phases**.

When the Moon is behind the Earth, fully reflecting the Sun, we see it as a **full moon**. When it's between the Earth and Sun, its illuminated side is facing away from us, so we can't see it at all. We call this a **new moon**. At right angles to the Earth and Sun, we can only see half of the Moon's lit-up half – hence, we see a **half-moon**. And at the angles in between, we see it as a **crescent** (when less than half of the lit-up surface is visible) or a fat **gibbous** moon (when between half and all is visible)

Have a look at the picture below, and it should all make sense.

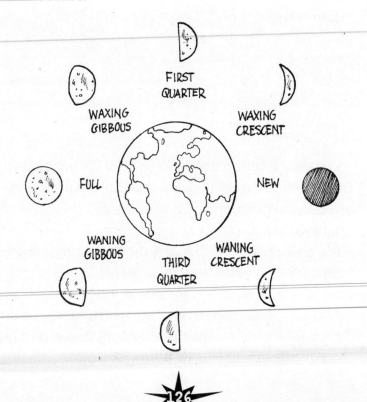

Spotting Moon shapes

Tonight, and for the few weeks, make a quick sketch of what shape the Moon is. Once you have a few weeks' worth of moon shapes, put them together like a comic strip to see how the moon waxes (becomes fully lit after a new moon) and wanes (gradually winks out between full moon and new moon). You'll notice it always waxes and wanes the same way.

Now look again at the diagram on page 125, and think about where the Moon was relative to the Earth and Sun each time, and what made it that shape. From now on, whenever you look at the Moon, you'll recognize whether it's waxing or waning, and whereabouts it is in Space, relative to the Earth and Sun. Get good at it, and you can even use it as a rough calendar to count the days of the month, just as the ancient astronomers all around the world once did.

Let's see your mates figure all *that* out!

Hang on a minute – I'm confused. If the Moon is right behind the Earth, how can we see it at all? And when it's between the Sun and the Earth, doesn't that make an eclipse?

Well spotted. It does partly disappear when it's *right* behind the Earth (which is called a **lunar eclipse**). And it can cause an eclipse of the Sun (or **solar**

eclipse) when it's right in front of it. But most of the time this doesn't happen, because the Moon's orbit isn't in the same plane as the Earth's orbit around the Sun – it's tilted. So the Moon spends most of its time moving above or below the line between the Sun and Earth, and we can see it almost all the time (except for during new moons, as we already saw).

Occasionally, the Moon will cross directly in front of the Sun, causing a solar eclipse. But even when this does happen, it won't be visible from everywhere on Earth – only the places the Moon's shadow passes directly over will see a **total eclipse**, while a wider surrounding region may see a **partial eclipse**. During a partial eclipse, the Moon covers part, but not all, of the Sun – making it look as if the Sun is trying to swallow the Moon whole!

What's more, because the Moon orbits the Earth in an elliptical (rather than a circular) path, it moves closer to or further from us at different times. At its closest point in its orbit (which astronomers call

perigee), the Moon appears large enough to blot out the entire Sun. But at its most distant point (or **apogee**), it's almost 40,000 km further away, and appears much smaller in the sky. If it passes in front of the Sun at this time, it can't cover the Sun's entire disc, and leaves a glowing ring around the outside. This is called an **annular** (or ring) **eclipse** (see picture on previous page).

Wow! I'd like to see one of those.

If you want to see an eclipse, the box below lists the dates when they will be visible over the next decade. Just make sure you view it properly and safely, as looking directly at the Sun at any time (and especially just before or after an eclipse, when it doesn't seem so painfully bright, so it's easier to stare at) is very dangerous, and can permanently damage your eyes. Instead, follow the instructions in the box below, and make your own home-made eclipse-viewer.

TOTAL SOLAR ECLIPSES 2010 TO 2020

11 July 2010
13 November 2012
20 March 2015
9 March 2016
21 August 2017
2 July 2019
14 December 2020

Not all of these will be visible in your part of the world. Check the NASA solar eclipse page (http://eclipse.gsfc. nasa.gov/solar.html) for details of where to see them.

Make your own pinhole projector to view eclipses

All you need is two bits of card – one with a small (1 mm) hole punched through the centre and held up to mask the Sun, the other held beneath. The Sun's image will appear on your DIY projector's 'screen' immediately.

IMAGE OF ECLIPSE

PIN HOLE

SUN BEHIND YOU

Lunar eclipses

*During a solar eclipse, the Moon shadows the Earth. But the opposite can happen too. When the Moon moves directly behind the Earth in the same plane, the Earth shadows the Moon, in what astronomers call a **lunar eclipse**.*

So then the Moon gets blacked out by the Earth's shadow and disappears?

Surprisingly, no. Instead, the Moon turns a deep red colour. This may also have been what the writers of the Bible's Old Testament were seeing when they described 'the Moon turning to blood'.

Yikes. That sounds a bit scary. So why does that happen?

Because, unlike the Moon, the Earth has an atmosphere. So even when it totally blocks the direct path of sunlight to the Moon, a little light is bounced (or refracted) through the thin veil of the Earth's atmosphere and strikes the Moon anyway. But remember what we said back in Chapter 3 about how white light can be split up into different colours when it's bounced or redirected? Well, the same thing happens here. As light from the Sun passes through the atmosphere, the blue end of the colour spectrum gets bounced out (making the atmosphere appear blue), while the red end of the spectrum makes it through and out the other side. So if the Moon happens to be in the way, it gets a temporary and dramatic red spotlight. Being a lifeless object, the Moon does not respond to this with a spontaneous song-and-dance routine, but, during a lunar eclipse, it certainly looks like it should.

Well, now we've whipped around the Earth, learned about atmospheres and seasons, and been eclipsed and mooned by the Moon, that concludes our tour of the Earth–Moon system.

So where to next, Captain?

* Do you want to head inwards, towards the centre of the solar system? Then turn to page 132 to set a course for **Venus**.
* Want to head outwards instead? Then turn to page 149 to set a course for **Mars**.

Venus

Earth's evil twin?

If you used enough sunscreen, could you sunbathe on Venus?

I for one wouldn't want to try it. Venus has hellish temperatures, hellish pressures, hellish winds and hellish rainstorms. To summarize: it's pretty hellish. No amount of sunscreen will keep you safe through all that.

CRUST

CORE

MANTLE

Come on. It can't be *that* bad.
Oh, believe me – it is.

Incredibly, astronomers once described Venus as the Earth's 'twin sister' in the solar system. You can understand their mistake. Venus is very similar in size, mass and density to the Earth. If it shared our home planet's orbit around the Sun, it would probably *look* very similar to the Earth too – with oceans and lakes lapping between its rolling hills and rocky landscape, and perhaps even living organisms going about their daily Venusian lives.

But because of its position closer to the Sun Venus receives far more heat, light and other forms of radiation than the Earth. This stronger 'grilling' has led to huge differences in the interior, surface and atmosphere of the two planets. And when the first

Space probe visited Venus almost fifty years ago, we quickly discovered that Venus was no twin of the Earth. Or, if it was, it was an evil one with a hellish environment.

What makes it so awful there?

In short, the atmosphere. Unlike the Moon, Venus is large enough to retain a gassy atmosphere with its gravity. But, unlike the Earth, it's not one you'd want to try breathing in.

You may recall that Earth's atmosphere is mostly nitrogen and oxygen, plus a little water vapour, and a tiny amount (less than 1 per cent) of the 'greenhouse' gas carbon dioxide. This keeps the surface temperature on Earth warm and toasty via the heat-trapping greenhouse effect.

Well, on Venus, the atmosphere is over 96 per cent carbon dioxide, less than 3 per cent nitrogen and there's no free oxygen or water vapour at all. Being slightly smaller (and a great deal hotter) than the Earth, the water-forming hydrogen gas on Venus has long since boiled off into Space, whilst the remaining oxygen became bound to sulphur and other elements.

What remains is just about the worst atmosphere you could ever hope to be in. Clouds of burning sulphuric acid rain down through thick, choking carbon dioxide gas – all held at a pressure ninety times greater than that of the Earth's atmosphere. To make matters worse, the runaway greenhouse effect caused by all the carbon dioxide gives Venus an average surface temperature of around 460°C (850°F).

So what would happen if you landed there and popped out of the spaceship for a stroll?

Nothing good, that's for sure. You'd be squashed flat by the immense pressures, suffocated by the toxic air, roasted alive by the oven-like temperatures and finally dissolved by the acid rain. Frankly, not much would remain to indicate that you'd ever been there at all.

Ah. Won't be building our new off-planet home here, then.

Probably not. Even if it wasn't hotter than we could stand, without water or breathable air, there's little hope of maintaining life on Venus, and astrobiologists (scientists who study and seek out extraterrestrial life) have long since given up on finding any native Venusian organisms. But there are a few things that make Venus interesting.

It has immense impact craters flooded and flattened with lava flows – hints of its fiery, volcanic past. It orbits the Sun once every 225 days, making the Venusian year 4.5 months shorter than an Earth year. And, unlike the Earth, it takes *243 days* to turn *once* on its axis . . . and, what's more, it spins *backwards* when compared to all the other planets (except Uranus, which not only spins backwards, but also sideways – more on that later). The combined effect of its faster orbit and super-slow backwards spin is that it takes 117 Earth days for any single point on Venus to circle once and face the Sun. In other words, the Venusian day is 117 Earth days long!

Ever feel like a day at school seemed to last for months? Well, if you went to school on Venus, it *would*.

Plus it'd be really hot all the time. And you could never go outside to do P.E. . . . .

Err . . . right. Also true.

Like the Moon, Venus also has phases – appearing fully lit, half-lit or crescent-shaped at different times. Gallileo (remember him?) first spotted these phases with his telescopes in 1610. This was important, because it provided more evidence for the heliocentric (Sun-centred) solar system – as the different phase pattern to the Moon suggested that Venus (at least) could not be orbiting the Earth.

And, perhaps most importantly of all, Venus gives us a glimpse of what the Earth could look like if the greenhouse effect were allowed to run out of control. Although our atmosphere could probably never get that thick with carbon dioxide, our hellish 'twin planet' stands as a warning of what could happen to our environment if we don't take steps to look after it.

And on that jolly note it's off we go again.
Where to next?

✳ If you're on your way towards the Sun, then turn to page 137 for the innermost planet, **Mercury**.

✳ If you've just come from Mercury and you've now seen all the planets, turn to page 179 for a final whizz through the system to visit the **dwarf planets**, **comets** and **asteroid belts**.

Mercury

The moon-sized metallic mini-planet!

Is Mercury actually made of mercury?
No, it isn't. Although it is mostly made of metal, the planet Mercury got its name before the metal did. Like most of the other planets, Mercury got its English name from an ancient god in Roman mythology. And as you might expect from a giant red-hot ball-bearing, it's not a very inviting place to live.

The pipsqueak of the solar system, Mercury is both the smallest and the closest planet to the Sun. At just 4,800 km across, Mercury is less than half the size of the Earth, and not much bigger than the Moon. In fact, it's actually smaller than several of the moons that orbit Jupiter and Saturn. And with its dusty, crater-faced surface and no atmosphere to speak of, Mercury looks pretty similar to the Moon too. Quite frankly, it's lucky it gets to call itself a planet at all.

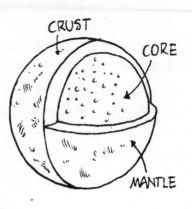

Mercury orbits the Sun at a distance of between 47 and 71 million km, tracing out the most elliptical (or least circular*) path of all the planets. But even at its furthest from the Sun, it's still less than half as far from the Sun as the planet Earth. It takes just eighty-eight days to lap the Sun, but rotates very slowly, taking fifty-eight Earth days to complete a single spin on its axis.

Arghhh! That sounds like a nightmare! You'd be doing tests every day. Plus it would be even hotter there, right?

Well, not really. But, in fact, it would be even less comfortable going to school on Mercury than it would on Venus. Being much closer to the Sun, you might think that it would be much hotter. But while surface temperatures on Mercury do climb almost as high (to 450°C, or 840°F) during the daytime, it swings wildly down to -150°C (-238°F) at night. This is because Mercury, like the Moon, lacks an atmosphere to hold the heat. So, as soon as it turns away from the Sun, the surface starts to lose heat and freeze.

Although with a day lasting about two months of an Earth year, at least you'd have time to change from your sun-shorts into your Arctic anorak. I'm joking, of course – even with the proper gear, you could *never* survive temperatures that hot or cold.

---

* Had they known this, Aristotle and Ptolemy, with all their love for prefect circles, would have *hated* Mercury.

I knew that. But if you _could_ survive the temperatures on Mercury, what would it be like to live there?

Not much more fun than the Moon, I'm afraid. Mercury is basically a barren, pock-marked, rock-covered ball-bearing in Space – with a thick core of solid iron and nickel overlaid with a thinner, molten-rock mantle and a crusty surface. Being larger than the Moon, it has a little more surface gravity, and about a third that of the Earth. So you could do a few high leaps and jumps, I suppose. But other than that there really wouldn't be much to do. No life, no water, no atmosphere. Not exactly Party Planet Central.

Right. That does it. This place is boring. Let's get out of here.

Okay. Where to next?

❊ If you're on your way inwards, towards the centre of the system, then grab your shades and tanning lotion, and turn to page 140. Next stop: **the Sun**.

❊ If you've just come from the Sun and you're heading out to see more, turn to page 132 to explore the planet **Venus**.

The Sun

Is it getting hot in here, or is it just me?

Will we ever set foot on the Sun?

No. Never. Not only is the surface of the Sun hotter than you can possibly imagine, but you'd most likely never make it through the Sun's outer halo to reach it. And even if you did there would be nothing to stand on.

Eh? Hold on – you've lost me there. What do you mean 'nothing to stand on'? And since when did the Sun have a halo?

Okay, let's roll this back a bit. First, here's the low-down on the Sun itself.

Strange as it may seem, the only true star of our solar system is a middle-aged dwarf.

What?

I'm serious. As we learned in the last chapter, the Sun (it has no official astronomical name, but is sometimes given its ancient Roman name, Sol) is a class G yellow dwarf star that is roughly 4.6 billion years old, which puts it a bit under halfway through its estimated 10-billion-year lifespan. We also learned that compared to other stars, such as blue supergiants, the Sun is fairly small, and not that hot or bright. But when you try to get your head around the sizes and temperatures involved, you soon see that the Sun is no less impressive for that.

The Sun contains 99.85 per cent of all the mass in the solar system*, weighing in at roughly 2 x 10²⁷ (or 2,000,000,000,000,000,000,000,000,000) tonnes. It's almost *impossible* for us to imagine something as massive as this. On a giant pair of weighing scales, you'd have to put 330,000 Earths on the other side to balance it out. But because it is four times less dense, it would take up a great deal more space. In terms of volume, you could fit roughly 1.3 million Earth-sized planets inside the Sun. So, in a way, the Sun is very heavy, but also very big and fluffy . . .

The Sun is also the source of heat and light in the entire solar system, belting out around 4 x 10²⁶ (or 400,000,000,000,000,000,000,000,000) Watts of power – equivalent to *4 trillion-trillion* lightbulbs!

Whoa. That's pretty hefty. So how hot does it get?
Well, that depends on which bit of the Sun you're talking about. Unlike the rocky planets, the Sun doesn't have strictly separated layers, as its gassy structure kind of blends them together. But for convenience astronomers divide the 'body' of the Sun into three major zones. At the 'surface' layer, called the photosphere, temperatures reach about 5,500°C (10,000°F). In the convection zone beneath, they reach

---

* Jupiter contains another 0.1 per cent, and the remaining 0.05 per cent is split between *all* the other planets, moons and objects!

2 million °C (3.6 million °F). Beneath that lies the radiative zone, and temperatures there reach up to 7 million °C (12 million °F). And right in the centre of the Sun, within the fusion core, it may reach 15 million °C (27 million °F) or more.

So you could never walk on the surface, not even if you had a special sun-proof suit or something?
Almost certainly not, I'm afraid. Even the strongest heat-proof suits (the kind that some volcano researchers and firefighters wear) only protect you up to about 1,000°C (1,800°F), so would melt away the instant you set foot in the photosphere. Not that you could actually 'set foot' on the Sun, either. Being a giant gas ball, the Sun has no solid surface to stand on, so if you tried you'd fall right into it. When we talk about the Sun's 'surface' we're really talking about the layer from which most of the visible light comes from, which for us outlines the Sun's circular shape (hence, it's called the *photosphere*, meaning 'light-ball').

Besides, even if you did have a spaceship and spacesuit that could withstand the thousands of degrees at the Sun's 'surface', you'd have to travel through its atmosphere first – parts of which are a great deal hotter.

The Sun's halo

The Sun's atmosphere extends for 6,000 miles (10,000 km) or more into Space, and has two layers – the

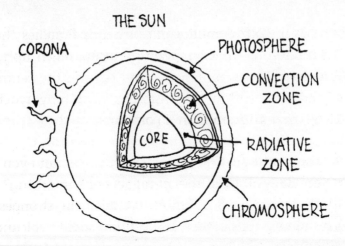

THE SUN

CORONA

PHOTOSPHERE

CONVECTION ZONE

RADIATIVE ZONE

CORE

CHROMOSPHERE

chromosphere and the corona. Both contain a range of gases at low densities, and both are normally invisible to us down here on Earth, appearing briefly only during an eclipse. This is because the photosphere beneath is much, much brighter, and outshines the dimmer atmosphere. But when the Moon temporarily shades out the photosphere during a total solar eclipse, the chromosphere and corona appear as a beautiful, fiery halo.

The chromosphere ('colour-ball') extends 1.2–1.8 miles (2,000–3,000 km) from the Sun's surface, and temperatures here range from 4,000–8,000°C (7,000–14,000°F). Outside this, the corona ('crown') is more wild and variable. Huge flaming spikes (or spicules) formed in the photosphere project through it and extend for 3.7–6.2 miles (6,000–10,000 km) into Space, whipped up by shifts in the Sun's immense magnetic field. Temperatures in this outer layer of the atmosphere can reach over 1 million °C (1.8 million °F) – over a thousand times those on the Sun's surface.

Hang on a minute – how can the bit furthest from the Sun be hotter than the surface? Wouldn't it get cooler the further away from the Sun you get? Where does all that heat come from?

That's a very good question. It's one that stumped astronomers for decades, but we now think we have the answer.

We know that the Sun's heat and energy originally come from powerful nuclear reactions happening within. Inside the Sun's fusion core, hydrogen atoms (or rather bits of them) are forced together at immense pressures and temperatures, and fuse to create atoms of the heavier elements deuterium and helium. This fusion process releases huge amounts of atomic energy, and is similar to that which goes on in some types of nuclear power plant on Earth – only the Sun has trillions of times more fuel to work with.

Okay . . .

Now the Sun's mass is about 70 per cent hydrogen, 28 per cent helium and 2 per cent other elements left over from the explosion of a nearby star or stars. Like all young stars, the Sun is slowly burning through its hydrogen 'fuel' and converting it to helium, producing massive amounts of energy. This is what creates the 15-million-degree temperatures in the fusion core. This energy then passes through the convection and radiative zones to the photosphere. From there, most of it radiates out into Space in the form of heat, light and other forms of radiation – warming the surfaces and atmospheres of planets, along with moons, asteroids, comets and other objects throughout the solar system. In general, the further from the Sun the planet or object is, the less radiation it will receive, and the colder it will be.

If this were the whole story, then the inner part of the Sun's own atmosphere (the chromosphere) should be cooler than the surface, and the outer part (the corona) should be cooler still. But as we now know, the corona is not only hotter than the chromosphere, it's also *thousands of times* hotter than the surface.

Right. So what gives?
One thing that could help explain it is that some energy also passes from the Sun's surface directly into its outer atmosphere, through special magnetic waves called Alfven waves. Astrophysicist Hannes Alfven first predicted the existence of these over sixty years ago, but they've only actually been spotted – using special equipment – very recently. They're created as the Sun spins and twists its magnetic field, snapping and breaking parts of the field and producing energy-carrying waves that extend for thousands of kilometres into Space. These Alfven

waves act as shortcuts that channel energy into the corona, heating it up to a million degrees or more. That's one reason why you'd have trouble getting to the Sun's surface to walk on it – the corona and chromosphere would frazzle you long before you got there.

Wait a minute – the Sun *spins*, like the planets do? I thought it just . . . you know . . . *sat* there.
Nope. It spins all right. It completes about one turn on its axis each month, but, unlike the more solid planets, different parts of the Sun rotate at different speeds*. At the equator, a full lap takes twenty-five days, but nearer the top and bottom, it takes more like thirty-six days. It's doing a gigantic twist, leading from the middle. And this is part of what pulls its magnetic field about to create weird effects like Alfven lines.

But it always looks the same to me. I've never seen the Sun spin or twist . . .
Ah, but astronomers have. Galileo was one of the first astronomers to describe sunspots** on the Sun, which eventually clued astronomers in to the movement

---

* Remember – unlike the rocky planets, the Sun isn't a solid ball. It's more like a huge, 3D whirlpool in Space – only it's made of gas instead of water.

** Although Chinese astrologers may have observed them a thousand years earlier.

of its surface. Sunspots are dark, cool patches on the Sun's surface caused by shifts in its magnetic field. By the late nineteenth century, astronomers had figured out that these spots appeared in cycles, and that tracking their movements upon the surface could reveal its rotation.

Sunspots also provided visible evidence of the Sun's powerful (but otherwise invisible) magnetic field, which also leads to other strange phenomena like **solar wind** and **solar flares**.

What are they, then?

The solar wind is a stream of charged particles which is flung outwards from the Sun by the loops and lines of its magnetic field. The stream of particles whizzes through Space at over 2,200 mph (3,600 km per hour), smashing into objects throughout the solar system. When they hit the icy body of an orbiting comet, they blast bits of dust and ice from it, creating its beautiful trailing 'tail'. When they reach our planet, they're channelled to the north and south poles by the Earth's own magnetic field. There, they collide with air molecules and create the beautiful, swirling coloured flashes we know as the northern and southern lights. Astronomers called them auroras.

Solar flares are a bit different. These are eruptions of matter from the Sun's surface, which occasionally blast forth from areas close to sunspots when magnetic field lines shift and break. Within a few minutes, a single solar flare can release more energy in the form of heat and charged particles than thousands of nuclear missiles. When flares happen, they cause spectacular auroras on Earth, and may even knock out orbiting satellites and electronic devices. A giant solar flare could, in theory, wipe out all life on the planet – although there's no evidence that's ever happened before, so we seem safe enough.

At our distance from the Sun, flares rarely cause us any danger. But in a spaceship flying within a few hundred thousand kilometres of the Sun itself, we're in serious peril. So let's not hang about.

Right. Time to make a swift exit.
Where to next?

⁕ If you've already explored the outer reaches of the solar system beyond Earth, then turn to page 137 to zip out to the next-closest planet to the Sun, **Mercury**.

⁕ Otherwise, turn to page 149 to set a course for **Mars** and beyond.

Mars

Red rocks and robot rovers!

Is there life on Mars . . . or what?

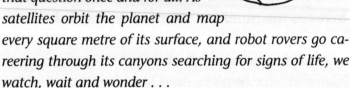

Despite many years of hoping and wondering about it, we're finally in a position to answer that question once and for all. As satellites orbit the planet and map *every square metre of its surface, and robot rovers go careering through its canyons searching for signs of life, we watch, wait and wonder . . .*

So is there?

Is there what?

Is there life on Mars?

Ah, yes. Of course. 'Is there life on Mars?'

Yeah. So is th—

. . . So sang famous musician David Bowie. Over the years, plenty of people have seemed to think so. In 1863, Italian priest and astronomer Angelo Secchi, observed Mars through his telescope and saw pictures of grooves or channels (in Italian, *canali*) on its surface. This sparked a rush of interest in the possibility of Martian life that was to last for many years. In 1894,

American astronomer Percival Lowell used his observatory in Arizona to study Mars more closely. From his observations, he mapped hundreds of 'canals' that he thought might have been built by a Martian civilization to transport water from the ice caps to the rest of the planet. By now, the world had Martian fever.

Grrrr . . . I wish you'd get on with it.
In 1898, H. G. Wells wrote his famous book *War of the Worlds* (more recently made into a movie with Tom Cruise) in which Martians attacked the Earth using giant war machines. Throughout the 1950s, evil Martians attacked the Earth over and over again in movies like *Invaders From Mars* (1953) and *It! The Terror From Beyond Space!* (1958). Then in 1971, David Bowie asked if there was 'Life on Mars' in his chart-topping song of the same name.

SO IS THERE?
Is there what?

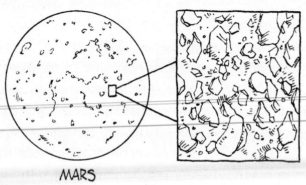

MARS

LIFE ON MARS?
Oh. No.

Gaaggh!
Well, certainly not the kind that can build canals
and invade the Earth, anyway. And in all likelihood
there's no life on Mars at all. Not even a measly patch
of lichen on its barren red rocks, or a single, slimy
bacterium.

That, frankly, is a bit of a let-down.
Indeed. In fact, the whole history of Mars exploration has been marked with let-downs and disappoint-
ments. Here's a summary of the major events (and
this isn't even all of them):

Missions to Mars
1960   Mars probe 1960A launched by the former
        Soviet Union. Doesn't even reach Earth
        orbit. **FAIL**.
1960   Mars probe 1960B is launched, four days
        later. Also wipes out. **FAIL**.
1962   The optimistically named Soviet 1962B Mars
        Lander also fails to leave the Earth. Again,
        FAIL.
1964   USA Space probe Mariner 3 attempts Mars
        fly-by, but fails when solar panels refuse
        to open. It now orbits the Sun instead,
        having missed its initial target by roughly

141 million miles (or 230 million km).
MEGA-FAIL.

1964   Mariner 4 passes within 3.7 miles (6 km) of Mars and takes the first close-up photos of its surface. **RESULT!**

1969   Mariners 6 and 7 pass even closer, taking measurements and hundreds more pics. Mariners 4, 6 and 7 eventually all end up in orbit around the Sun, presumably to make Mariner 3 feel better about itself. **RESULT!**

1969   Meanwhile, in the Soviet Union, two more Mars probes fail to make it off the launch pad. **FAIL**.

1971   The Soviet Mars 2 Orbiter/Soft Lander fails to orbit or land softly, as its rocket-brakes fail and it crashes into the surface of Mars. **EPIC FAIL**.

1972   NASA's Mariner 9 Orbiter arrives in Mars orbit during a planet-wide dust storm, but still manages to snap photographs of Phobos and Diemos, the Martian moons, and discovers some new 'river-like' channels on Mars. Although long since inactive, it's still up there orbiting Mars today. **PARTIAL SUCCESS**.

1975   NASA's Viking 1 and Viking 2 probes successfully land on Mars, map its surface, take soil samples and search for bacterial life. No life found, but, in all, **RESULT!**

1992   NASA's Mars Observer fails to observe Mars, as communication with it is lost before it enters Mars orbit. **FAIL**.

1996   NASA Mars Global Surveyor makes up for it by getting there and mapping the surface, which it continues to do  to this day. This is shortly followed by the Mars Pathfinder – the first successful robot rover to land on Mars. **RESULT!**

1998   Japan's Nozomi (meaning 'hope') probe has a communication malfunction before entering Mars orbit. The Japan Space programme literally loses Hope, and cries, 'DA-ME!' ('**FAIL!**')

1999   NASA Mars Polar Lander is destroyed on impact. **FAIL**.

2003   The European Space Agency's Mars Express makes good time to Mars, but its Beagle2 landing craft fares less well, doing a high-speed face-plant on the surface. **EURO-FAIL**.

2004   NASA Mars Exploration Rovers (MERs) Spirit and Opportunity arrive safely on Mars and begin their continuing data-finding joyride around the planet. **SUCCESS!**

While the two rovers and the Mars Global Surveyor have failed to find any signs of life, they have managed to tell us a great deal about the Martian surface and atmosphere. So after thirty years of trying we haven't found any signs of life. But we have discovered a lot of other stuff about our rusty, red planetary neighbour.

So what's it really like there?
Mars is a dry, dusty desert of a planet. Or rather a *rusty* desert, since its red colour comes from metal oxides on its surface – the same stuff you get on a rusty bike or car.

It's the last of the **Terrestrial Planets** – the four dense, rocky planets closest to the Sun, the other members of the group being Mercury, Venus and Earth. Mars is just over half the size of Earth, and spins on its axis at roughly the same rate – once every 24.6 hours. Its atmosphere, however, makes it a lot more like a chilly Venus than a smaller, drier Earth. Like that of Venus, the Martian atmosphere is over 96 per cent carbon dioxide, together with small amounts of nitrogen and a tiny amount of oxygen. And although it is held at a much lower pressure and temperature, it would still be toxic and unbreathable for humans. And with surface temperatures on Mars swinging from a toasty 26°C (80°F) to a freezing -125°C (-194°F), it's not the most hospitable place for an extraterrestrial Space colony (more on those in

Chapter 6). But it's not necessarily the worst place for one, either.

If we do one day manage to land on Mars and form some sort of base there, the scenery would make it a lot more worthwhile than living on the Moon. Not much to see on the Moon, after all. But Mars has two moons of its own, **Phobos** and **Deimos**, plus the largest mountains and canyons anywhere in the solar system.

Olympus Mons, an extinct volcano and the largest mountain on Mars, is **15 miles** (24 km) **high** and **310 miles** (500 km) **wide**. That's over three times taller and wider than Mount Everest on Earth. Alone, it could cover most of southern England, or all of the Hawaiian islands. The great rift valley on Mars, **Valles Marineris**, dwarfs America's Grand Canyon. It's over **3,000 miles** (5,000 km) **long**, and up to **62 miles** (100 km) **wide**. On Earth, it would stretch right across the United States.

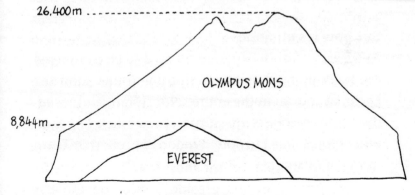

That's pretty cool. But . . .
But . . .

. . . but nothing lives there, and nothing ever has?
Well, we don't know that for sure. According to information recently beamed back by the NASA's Opportunity robot rover, it's too dry and salty on the surface for even bacterial life to survive. But there is evidence – including canyons, ravines and dried-up riverbeds – that water once flowed on the planet. So a long time ago Mars may have been wetter, warmer and a possible home for Martian life. Scientists now think that beneath the Martian ice caps – made mostly from frozen carbon dioxide – there may be massive amounts of frozen water. Some estimate that as much as half of each ice cap may in fact be made of water. If this much water existed, and it somehow melted, it would create an **ocean** in Mars's northern hemisphere. And maybe, at one time, there *was* a Martian ocean. Possibly teeming with aquatic Martian life.

But now it's all gone.
As far as we can tell, yes. Mars used to be considered the most probable place to find life (other than the Earth, of course) in the entire solar system. But nowadays astrobiologists are starting to pin their hopes on other places, like **Europa** (a moon of Jupiter) or **Titan** (a moon of Saturn).

Well, what are we waiting for?
Eh? What do you mean?

Let's go and look there, then!
Fair enough. Buckle up – now leaving Mars orbit.
*Next stop: **Jupiter**.*

Jupiter

The Solar System's Big Daddy.

How many Earths could fit inside Jupiter?

*Jupiter is the giant of the solar system, being by far the largest planet within it. Jupiter has over **318***

The diagram shows Jupiter's internal structure with labels: MOLECULAR HYDROGEN, CORE, LIQUID METALLIC HYDROGEN.

times the mass of the Earth, and twice the mass of all the other planets in the solar system combined. But because it's far less dense than the Earth, it's way bigger than 318 Earths in terms of volume. In fact, you could fit about **1,300 planet Earths** inside Jupiter's hulking body.

So Jupiter is way bigger and heavier than the Earth, but isn't quite as solid?

Right. Jupiter is the first of the four **Jovian Planets**, which are separated from the four **Terrestrial Planets** by an **asteroid belt**, and include Jupiter, Saturn, Uranus and Neptune. Like the other Jovian planets, Jupiter is a gas giant – a planet composed more of gas than of solid or liquid rock. It's made of roughly 97 per cent hydrogen and helium, plus small amounts of methane, ammonia, water and other chemical compounds.

Weird. That sounds more like the Sun than a planet.

You're right – in many ways, it is. In fact, astronomers

think Jupiter probably still looks a lot like the gas cloud (or **stellar nebula**) that the Sun and solar system formed from billions of years ago – it has just clotted into a sphere and taken on a more defined shape. And, just like the Sun, Jupiter has no surface that you can land on or walk on. The 'surface' we see when we look at it through telescopes is actually just the top layer of clouds swirling above the liquid hydrogen that makes up most of its body*.

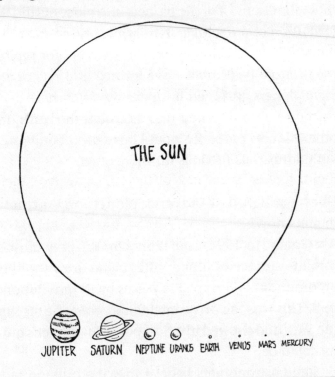

THE SUN

JUPITER   SATURN   NEPTUNE URANUS EARTH VENUS MARS MERCURY

---

* In fact, Jupiter's famous 'red spot' is actually a system of swirling storm clouds – like a permanent hurricane over 40,000 km across. That's almost three times wider than the entire Earth!

However, make no mistake – Jupiter may be gassy, but it's no airy-fairy lightweight. You could fit eleven planet Earths side by side across its equator, and its huge gravitational pull is so powerful that it affects planets as far away as Mercury and Neptune, and regularly pulls comets and asteroids towards the inner part of the solar system from the vast clouds of rock floating outside it.

In fact, astronomers think that Jupiter's enormous mass shoved most of the planets into place during the formation of the solar system, while preventing other planets from forming at all. If it were not for Jupiter, the asteroid belt might have formed into one or two *more* planets. But then if Jupiter were not there to attract and absorb comets and asteroids, the Earth and other planets probably would have been bombarded with dangerous fireballs far more often.

Does it still pull at the other planets and attract comets now?

Absolutely. In 1994, comet Shoemaker-Levy crashed into the surface of Jupiter after being drawn into orbit around it and ripped to pieces by its gravitational pull. This was the first comet found not to be orbiting the Sun, and showed just how powerful Jupiter's gravity could be.

Some astronomers believe that the hulking mass of Jupiter could one day wreck the whole solar system. It is already pulling Mercury into a wider, more stretched orbit each year, and one day it could send Mercury reeling into the Sun (bad), into Venus (worse) or even into the Earth (really not good at all). If this happened, it would destroy all life on the planet, and make previous asteroid impacts look like pinpricks. Both planets would smash into partially liquefied smithereens, leaving very little behind to show that we ever existed.

Yikes!
But don't worry – there's only a 1 per cent chance that this will happen before the Sun swells up into a red giant and frazzles both planets anyway.

Oh. Well, that's just *great*.
Another result of Jupiter's enormous mass is that it has moons. *Lots* of them. As we saw in Chapter 2, Galileo spotted the first (and largest) four – Ganymede, Callisto, Io and Europa – way back in 1610. But within the last thirty years, astronomers and Space probes like NASA's Voyager have discovered over **fifty more** moons, twenty of them

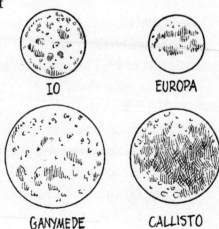

IO

EUROPA

GANYMEDE

CALLISTO

discovered between 2001 and 2002 alone! So Jupiter now has sixty-three moons, and still counting.

Sixty-three? Wow. So could we make a moon base on one of those? And do any have life on them?
Maybe so. It's certainly possible. And as we'll see in the final chapter, Europa, in particular, is a strong candidate for both bacterial life and – in the distant future – manned exploration. But more about that later.

Cool! I like Jupiter. Jupiter rocks.
Here's one more cool thing about it. Jupiter, like Saturn, also has a **ring**. The Voyager 1 probe discovered this in 1979, when it turned around to take one final snapshot of Jupiter before moving on to Saturn. It came as quite a surprise. But we now know that *all* the Jovian gas giant planets have ring systems.

They do?
Yep. Some have rings of ice, and others rings of rock. But Uranus and Neptune sport their own stylish rings too.

But none, perhaps, are as impressive as the rings of Saturn, which have fascinated astronomers since the time of Galileo. It's also, coincidentally, where we're off to next. So buckle up cos we're off to the 'planet with the bling'.

*Next stop: **Saturn**.*

Saturn

Giant with a halo . . .

What are Saturn's rings made of?

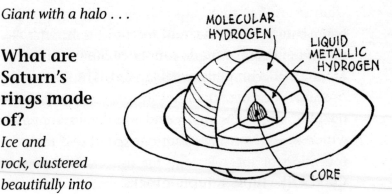

MOLECULAR HYDROGEN

LIQUID METALLIC HYDROGEN

CORE

Ice and rock, clustered beautifully into circular rows and lanes, which are helpfully held in place by the orbit of Saturn's 'shepherd moons'. Saturn's rings have fascinated astronomers for centuries since the time of Galileo. But only recently, after sending Space probes to take a closer look, have we come to understand how and why they formed.

So Galileo spotted them first?

Right. But he couldn't explain what he was seeing.

Fifty years after Galileo first spotted what he described as 'ears' on the planet Saturn, Dutch astronomer Christiaan Huygens suggested that it was actually a ring around the entire planet, rather than ears, handles or bulges on either side. He also discovered the first and largest of Saturn's many moons, **Titan**, which today holds almost as much interest for astronomers as the planet Saturn itself.

The second gas giant in the solar system, Saturn

has much the same make-up as Jupiter, and it is almost as large (9.5 Earths would fit across its equator, rather than Jupiter's 11-Earth width). But being much less dense, and lacking the heavier elements in its core, its mass is 'only' about 95 times that of the Earth, compared with Jupiter's 318.

Saturn was also the last planet known to ancient peoples, since it is the most distant of the planets which is easily visible to the naked eye. It took the invention of the telescope for astronomers to spot the barely-visible Uranus and the invisible Neptune beyond. Saturn rotates very quickly on its axis, completing a full spin in just over ten hours, but at its huge distance away, it takes almost thirty years to orbit the Sun.

Never mind all that, what about the rings?
Right. The most stunning features of this planet are, of course, its rings. Seven major rings (labelled with

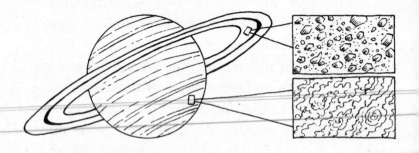

letters from A to G) encircle the planet, stretching to a distance of over 300,000 miles (480,000 km) from the surface. That's over twice the width of Saturn itself, and about 1.5 times the distance from the Earth to the Moon!

Wow! That's some pretty big bling.

Right. But, unfortunately, these rings aren't made of solid silver or gold. Instead, they're made up of billions of balls of ice or icy rock, ranging in size from microscopic specks to house-sized boulders. And, although it may not look like it, these chunks are so spread out that if you squashed them all together their total 298,000-mile (480,000-km) width could be compressed into a solid ring just a few metres across. It also means that you could easily fly a large spacecraft straight through them without hitting anything.

Smart! I'd love to try doing that.

You'd have to take care, however, not to accidentally hit one of Saturn's moons. Like Jupiter, Saturn has more than **sixty** of them. Most of these are little more than immense chunks of ice, like dirty snowballs orbiting the planet. But a few, like **Titan**, **Enceladus** and **Mimas**, are more rocky and volcanic (though these volcanoes produce ice not lava). Some, like

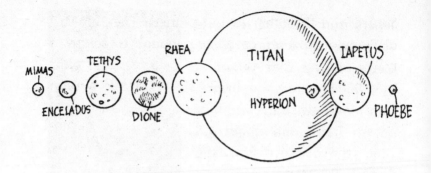

MIMAS   ENCELADUS   TETHYS   DIONE   RHEA   TITAN   HYPERION   IAPETUS   PHOEBE

Titan, orbit outside of the rings. Others, like **Atlas**, **Prometheus** and **Pandora**, are so-called **shepherd moons**. These orbit above, below or within the rings – clearing paths between them, sculpting the rings' edges, and helping to hold their shape.

Where did the rings come from? Have they always been there?

We don't think so, no. The rings are very old, but it seems that they may once have been a moon (or a group of several moons) that was ripped apart by Saturn's huge gravitational pull, or possibly disintegrated by the impact of a comet or asteroid.

The rings are made of smashed moons? Brilliant!

We think so, yes. It seems that after a moon is broken up like this most of the remaining bits and pieces would naturally be drawn into a ring shape by the planet's gravity, with perhaps some bits coming back together to form new moons later on. That would explain the presence of both moons and rings around

Saturn and the other Jovian planets. The Terrestrial Planets, however, aren't big enough to create or maintain ring systems like this. So Earth and Mars may have moons, but they seem destined to remain ring-less.

A MOON GETS TOO CLOSE TO SATURN'S SURFACE AND IS RIPPED APART BY ITS TIDAL FORCES...

THE MOON BREAKS UP INTO ICY/ROCKY CLUMPS, CIRCLING THE PLANET...

WHICH, OVER TIME, BREAK DOWN INTO SMALLER AND SMALLER PIECES... CREATING A RING

Shame. So what else do we know about Saturn?
Although a lot still remains to be discovered, NASA's Cassini-Hugyens probe, which arrived in 2004, has already revealed more information about Saturn, its rings and its moons than we've ever known before. Amongst other things, it has spotted oceans, lakes and sand dunes on Titan, icy plumes shooting from cryo-volcanoes on the surface of Enceladus and mysterious 'flying saucers' skimming between Saturn's rings.

Flying saucers? Like, real ones?
Don't get too excited. It turns out they were bits of smashed moon, left behind after moonlets orbiting within the ring system collided.

Oh. Well, that's still pretty cool.
The big draw for astrobiologists, though, is Titan. The atmosphere on Titan is similar to that on Earth billions of years ago, when life here first began. And many scientists now believe that there may be a massive ocean of liquid water beneath its 100-km icy crust. If so, it's possible that alien life of some sort could be lurking within. Maybe some extraterrestrial bacteria, or maybe something more advanced. Who knows.

But that's a story for another day. For now, we're off to explore the final two planets in the solar system.

Can we buzz through the rings on the way out? Pleeeeeeeeeeeeeeeeeeeeaaaaase?
Oh, all right, then. Here we go.

Wahey!
*Next stop: **Uranus**.*

Uranus

No one gets my name right.

Why does Uranus sound so rude?
It doesn't. Not if you say it right. It's pronounced 'YOR-ah-NUS', not – well . . . you know.

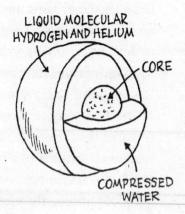

LIQUID MOLECULAR HYDROGEN AND HELIUM

CORE

COMPRESSED WATER

Heh heh heh heh. But it *sounds* like . . .
No, it doesn't. So you can stop all that snickering and chuckling. There's nothing rude about the seventh planet in our solar system. Although you could say Uranus is a 'funny planet' for other reasons . . .

Oh, all right. So why's it still 'funny', then?
Well, for starters it spins backwards. Most of the other planets rotate on their axes in the same direction they orbit the Sun – anti-clockwise. But Uranus (like Venus, as we've already seen) is unusual because it spins the opposite way. Astronomers call this **retrograde rotation**. And Uranus and Venus are the only two planets that do it.

Weird.
It gets weirder. Uranus takes just seventeen hours to

rotate once on its axis, which gives it a shorter day than the Earth. But the central axis of Uranus is tilted so far over (at 97.86 degrees, to be exact) it's more or less lying on its side. At one point in its eighty-four-year orbit, its north pole points almost directly towards the Sun. When it reaches the opposite side of the Sun forty-two years later, its south pole points towards the Sun instead. Viewed from above the solar system, Uranus looks almost as if it's *rolling* around the Sun – like a big snooker ball trundling along an invisible groove through Space.

That *is* a bit strange.
Stranger still, the seasons on Uranus only last for a day. Or rather, the days last for an entire season . . .

Eh? How does that work?
Well, if you think about it, tilting the planet over so that the poles lie flat means that the same bits of planet are exposed to (or shaded from) the Sun even while Uranus rotates. On Earth and the other planets, the planet's vertical spin creates day and night with every rotation, while seasons change as the planet slowly moves around the Sun. But as Uranus 'rolls' its way horizontally around the Sun, half the planet spins away in constant sunlight, while the other half spins in total darkness. For day to become night (and vice versa), the planet has to orbit halfway around the Sun, by which time it has also moved through

two of the four seasons. And by the time the 'lit' and 'shaded' halves switch back again, another two seasons have passed. So a single day on Uranus lasts for an entire summer, while a single night lasts all winter. How awful would that be?

Oh, I dunno. Not that bad. You could go tobogganing all night long . . .
. . . but then you'd have to get up for school the next day – which would last *all summer*.

Arghhhh!
Exactly. But other than that Uranus is still a pretty cool place. Cool, because it's mostly made of freezing

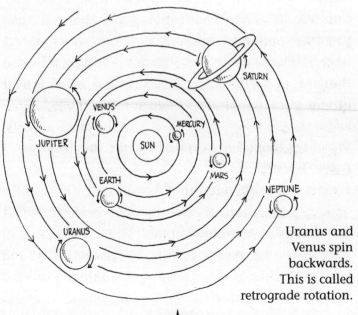

Uranus and
Venus spin
backwards.
This is called
retrograde rotation.

gaseous hydrogen, helium and water, surrounding a small, rocky core. Cool because it has a surface temperature which stays at around -200°C (-328°F) all year round. And cool because it also has over twenty-five moons and ten rings surrounding it. And just to be different (or awkward, perhaps) the rings on Uranus are vertical, rather than horizontal, like those of Saturn or Jupiter.

Smart! So how did Uranus end up like that? I mean, all sideways and stuff?
Well, as with much of the solar system, we can't say for sure. But many astronomers think Uranus may have been struck a glancing blow by another planet, comet, or asteroid, which bounced its axis of rotation into its current, horizontal state. Then Uranus's satellites (or moons) and ring systems – which at first were probably more like Saturn's – simply followed the lean of the axis and settled into a near-vertical orbit around the planet's sideways-tilted belly.

Wow! It's like a big game of cosmic marbles up there, isn't it?
I guess you could put it that way.

So where do we bounce to next?
That's an easy question. Only one planet left in the solar system.
  *Next stop: **Neptune.***

Neptune

Deep blue and distant . . .

Why is Neptune called Neptune? Is there an ocean there?

In ancient Roman mythology, Neptune was the god of the seas (the Greeks called him Poseidon).
When Neptune was first discovered in 1846, it was given that name because Neptune was one of the few major Roman gods* who didn't yet have a planet named after him. But – as NASA's Voyager 2 probe found out around 150 years later, the name turned out to fit the planet well.

LIQUID MOLECULAR HYDROGEN AND HELIUM

CORE

COMPRESSED WATER

So it does have an ocean, then?

Sadly, no. It's blue, but there its similarity to the ocean ends.

Neptune is a large, blue-coloured gas planet about the same size as sixty planet Earths, but with just seventeen times its mass. Its colour comes not from a deep blue sea, but from the methane gas in its upper

---

* The other Roman-god planets being **Venus** (the goddess of love), **Mercury** (messenger to the gods), **Mars** (the god of war), **Saturn** (the god of farming) and **Jupiter** (king of the gods). **Uranus**, once again, is the awkward one here – being named after a Greek god, rather than a Roman god. There's always one, isn't there?

atmosphere. Still, I'm sure Neptune would've been happy to live there. If it wasn't so cold, maybe.

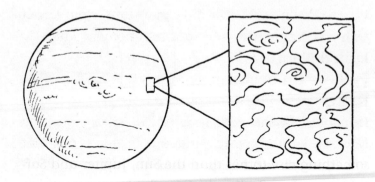

And they didn't know it was blue when they named it?
Nope. Actually, they could hardly see it at all. Before the Voyager 2 probe's 1986 fly-by, we knew almost nothing about Neptune besides the fact that it was . . . well . . . *there*. Like Uranus, Neptune was invisible to ancient astronomers, as you need a telescope to see it. But unlike Uranus, even *with* a powerful telescope, Neptune is still extremely difficult to see.

So how did they find it, then? I mean, if you can hardly see it even *with* a telescope, how did you even know it was there?
They used maths.

Maths?
Yep – maths. While Uranus was spotted by keen-

eyed astronomer William Herschel in 1781, even he couldn't make out Neptune with his telescope. That didn't happen until 1846, when French mathematician Urbain Le Verrier did some sums, figured out where Neptune was and told astronomers where to look for it.

Blimey. How'd he manage that?

He looked at the path of Uranus's orbit, and used Isaac Newton's gravity equations to figure out that something else (other than the Sun, Jupiter and Saturn) must be affecting it. Once he knew something was out there, with a few more swift calculations he also figured out how massive it must be, how far it was from the Sun and Uranus, and quickly calculated its orbit and expected position in the sky. He got it right, to within one degree of where it actually was. Less than three months later, German astronomer Johann Gottfried Galle followed Le Verrier's directions and spotted the real planet Neptune.

That was pretty clever of him.

Yep – very clever. In fact, this was the first planet that was predicted solely using mathematics, and only later discovered using real observations. But, ever since, astronomers have been using the same technique to find moons, asteroids and more. They even use it to find planets in other solar systems. But more on that later.

Have they found any moons around Neptune?

Yep. Loads of them. Like all the other Jovian planets, Neptune has multiple moons and rings. Its largest moon is called **Triton** (who, fittingly, was the son of Neptune in Roman mythology). Triton is an ice-covered planet which – like Saturn's moon Enceladus – is covered with active cryo-volcanoes and geysers that blast ice high into its atmosphere. Many astronomers think there may be liquid water (and possibly even life of some kind) beneath its surface, heated by the planet's hot, volcanic interior. But besides Triton, Neptune has at least twelve more moons, including five that were only discovered within the last decade.

So what's it like there?

Well, as you might expect for the distant outpost of the solar system, it's cold and lonely. Like Uranus, Neptune is pretty much a big ball of ice with a rocky core and a thin atmosphere of freezing hydrogen and helium. Even if you could set foot on its surface, you probably wouldn't want to for long. Like Uranus, its average surface temperature lurks at a bracing -200°C (-328°F). And its cloud systems are made of frozen methane and hydrogen sulphide – which makes the air smell like rotten eggs. Being on Neptune would probably be much like being in a freezer full of farts.

Ugh! Not heading there for my holidays, then.
I suppose not.

Is that it, then? Have we seen the whole solar system?
Not quite. That's all the planets done, but there's still more to see if you're up for it.

Like what?
Well, with one final whip around the outer reaches and back through the system, we can take in the rarer sights – like the dwarf planets, asteroid belts and comet clouds. How does that sound?

Brilliant! Let's go!
Okay. Then buckle up tight – it's full-speed to Pluto!

SEIDOKU (Planetary sudoku)

Play just like regular sudoku, except the numbers 1–9 have been replaced with the symbols for the Sun and the eight planets in the solar system. It might be tougher than you think!

Each horizontal and vertical line – and each square of nine squares – must contain all nine of the following symbols.

Key

☉	Sun	☿	Mercury	♀	Venus
⊕	Earth	♂	Mars	♃	Jupiter
♄	Saturn	♅	Uranus	Ψ	Neptune

	Ψ				⊕			
♅	☿	♀	♃	♂				☉
♂					♅		♀	
	⊕	♄		♅		Ψ		☿
	♀		☿		♃		☉	
☿		♂		⊕		♅	♄	
	♄		☉					♅
⊕				♀	♄	☉	Ψ	♃
			⊕				♂	

(answers on page 253)

Dwarf planets

Who'd have thought it?

Why doesn't Pluto get to be a planet any more?

Because astronomers have decided that it's neither big nor unique enough in our solar system. Faced with the discovery of many new Pluto-like objects, they were forced to choose between adding a load of new planets to the system, or calling Pluto and these newer objects something else. Unfortunately for Pluto, they chose option two.

It just doesn't seem right. When did all this happen, anyway?

For thousands of years, there were six planets known to star-gazers and astronomers. In 1781, that six became seven, with the discovery of Uranus. In 1846, seven became eight, with the official discovery of Neptune. Then in March 1930, American astronomer Clyde Tombaugh – after a long and laborious search – discovered **Pluto**.

Within the space of three centuries, our solar system had grown in size from six to nine planets. But just a few years ago, it dropped back to eight again. In 2006, strange as it may seem, we lost a planet. And that planet was poor old Pluto.

Pluto is a large ball of ice-covered rock found roughly 3.7 billion miles (5.9 billion km) from the Sun. By comparison, the Earth is roughly five times larger and 500 times heavier, and its surface gravity is twenty times stronger. Pluto takes 248 years to orbit the Sun in an oval orbit so stretched (or eccentric) that it sometimes passes inside that of Neptune. Shortly after its discovery, it was named by an eleven-year-old British girl called Venetia Burney, whose suggestion was picked from among thousands of others worldwide.

So did she name it after the Disney dog, then?
Actually, it was the other way around. Mickey Mouse's faithful friend, Pluto, didn't appear on screen until 1931, a whole year later. So the dog was named after the planet! This little girl knew her mythology and, like the other planets, Pluto's name comes from an ancient mythological character. In Greek mythology, Pluto (otherwise known as Hades) was the King of Hell, or the god of the underworld*.

So if it was even smaller than Neptune, how did they find it? More maths, or did someone just spot it one day?
A little of both. Astronomer Percival Lowell (remember him? The guy who thought there were alien waterways on Mars?) calculated the orbits of the eight known planets, and became convinced that there

---

* Charon, Pluto's largest moon, was named after the scary, skeletal boatman who used to ferry the souls of the dead across the River Styx and into Pluto's underworld. Creepy, eh?

was another one out there beyond Neptune. He gave it the mysterious moniker 'Planet X', and searched for it using the huge telescope at his own observatory. He died before he could find it, but the task then passed to young astronomer Clyde Tombaugh, who photographed and analyzed the positions of tens of thousands of stars in his search. Within a year, he had found it. As it turns out, he was very lucky – as Lowell's calculations were wrong, and there was no need for a Planet X to explain the motions of the first eight planets at all.

Well, he wasn't that lucky, was he? After all, his planet's not a planet any more. What's up with that?
Sadly, Pluto wasn't as unique as Lowell and Tombaugh thought. Pluto is just one of many objects orbiting the Sun at roughly the same distance. This is part of the reason why Tombaugh was able to spot it – far from being a mysterious loner, Lowell's 'Planet X' is just one of 200 or more similar objects forming a belt of large, rocky objects beyond the orbit of Neptune.

Once astronomers figured this out, they had to decide whether these new '**plutoids**', which they were discovering thick and fast, could *all* be called planets, or whether Pluto, along with these other objects, was really something else. And when astronomer Mike Brown discovered a plutoid (then called **Xena**, but now formally named **Eris**) which was *bigger* than Pluto, that pretty much spelled the end of it. Pluto the

181

planet was no more, and a new category of celestial object was born. The **dwarf planet**.

What makes a dwarf planet? Is it just smaller than a regular planet?

Partly, yes. Dwarf planets are a bit more than asteroids, and a bit less than a full-on planet. But it's also to do with how and where they're found in Space. Unlike an asteroid, a dwarf planet has to have cleared its path through Space of other objects. They do this by being large – ploughing them out of the way or by capturing them with their gravity – then either absorbing them or turning them into circling moons[*].

If a Sun-orbiting object is spherical (or near-spherical) and massive enough to clear its own orbital path through Space, it's classified as a dwarf planet. If it's smaller, more irregular in shape and exists alongside other objects in roughly the same path around the Sun, then it's classified as an **asteroid** or **small solar-system body**. Most – but not all – of the dwarf planets found so far exist in orbits beyond Neptune, in the region of Pluto. These are also known as **Trans-Neptunian Objects** (**TNOs**) or **plutoids**.

So how many dwarf planets are there?

So far, four have been recognized and named, including Pluto. But there are almost certainly many, many

---

[*] This, we now know, is how Pluto captured its moon Charon.

more out there that fit the bill, and are just waiting for official naming and recognition. Since there are likely to be more than eight of them, astronomers have resisted the urge to rename icy Pluto 'Snow White' and name the others after the seven dwarfs. Instead, they are usually named after gods or mythological figures, as many of the planets are.

So what are they called?
The first five recognized dwarf planets are **Pluto**, **Ceres**, **Eris**, **MakeMake** and **Haumea**. Pluto, we know all about already. Here's a bit about the others:

- **Ceres**, named after a Roman goddess, was previously classified as an asteroid, and lies in the wide **asteroid belt** between Mars and Jupiter. It was discovered in 1801, and recognized as *by far* the largest asteroid in the solar system. At almost 620 miles (1,000 km) across, it's roughly the same size as France. Its surface gravity is only a fifth that of Pluto, and a thirtieth that of the Earth, but is still strong enough to hold Ceres in a spherical shape. So it looks more like a mini-planet than an asteroid, and fits the dwarf-planet bill nicely.

- **Eris**, was discovered in January 2005, and temporarily named **UB313**, or **Xena**. At roughly 1,500 miles (2,500 km) across, it's actually a bit bigger than Pluto, so has more right to the dwarf-

CERES

ERIS

MAKEMAKE

HAUMEA

planet title. It also has it own moon, **Dysnomia**.
Eris sits in an orbit beyond Pluto, around 6.3 billion
miles (10 billion km) from the Sun, and takes 557
years to lap it (compared to Pluto's 248-year orbit).
It has an atmosphere of frozen methane and
nitrogen, giving it a slightly yellowish colour.

- **MakeMake** (pronounced *Ma-kay-Ma-kay*) was
discovered in March 2005, and named after a
Polynesian god of fertility. At roughly 1,000 miles
(1,600 km) across, it's about three-quarters of the
size of Pluto, and sits between Pluto and Eris at an
average distance of 4.8 billion miles (7.8 billion
km). It takes around 310 years to orbit the Sun.

- **Haumea** was discovered back in 2003, but was
more recently reclassified to become the fifth
dwarf planet, after much argument and debate
amongst astronomers. It rotates very quickly,
which has led astronomers to believe it was once
struck by another object, leaving it stretched out
and whizzing around the Sun. It's about 1,200
miles (2,000 km) long, but just 620 miles (1,000
km) wide, takes 285 years to orbit the Sun and has
two known moons – called **Hi'iaka** and **Namaka**.

Is that all of them, then?

That's all the dwarf planets that have been classified so far. But there are loads more known TNOs and plutoids – including four particularly large ones known as **Orcus, Sedna, Quaoar** and **Varuna** – and probably hundreds more out there waiting to be discovered. Some of these may eventually end up being reclassified as dwarf planets too. So the known solar system is expanding every day!

In addition, there are literally millions of smaller objects, such as asteroids and comets, orbiting the Sun at different distances throughout the system. And although they may never reach even dwarf planet status, they're still important and interesting to study. Not least because some of them threaten to whack into our planet one day . . .

One more question.

What?

Do dwarf planets have, like, dwarfs living on them?

Now you're just being silly.

Or elves, maybe? No, wait – then I guess they'd be elf planets . . .

Asteroids and Comets

Rockin' the solar system!

Where do comets and asteroids come from? Are they alien missiles?

Unlike the ones you see in the movies, most asteroids and comets whip about the Sun quite harmlessly. Only some have orbits that intersect with that of the Earth or other planets. And while it's worth watching out for them, we don't have to worry about them ploughing into us and destroying the planet just yet. And no – there's no one flinging them at us.

ASTEROID

ASTEROID WITH
LAYERED INTERIOR

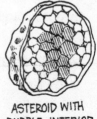

ASTEROID WITH
RUBBLE INTERIOR

Are you *sure* about that?

Yes, pretty sure. Unless you count the planet Jupiter. He does fling them at us from time to time.

Eh?

Let me explain.

The vast majority of asteroids in the solar system exist within two wide bands of Space – one between Mars and Jupiter, imaginatively named the **asteroid belt**, and the other stretching beyond the orbit of Neptune, in an area astronomers call the **Kuiper belt**. There are millions of asteroids spread between these two belts, but only a small number of them are occasionally pulled or bashed out of their regular orbits, to begin hurtling dangerously towards Earth and the innermost planets.

But aren't asteroid belts dangerous for spaceships and stuff?
Well, since we've never even made it to Mars, let alone beyond it to the asteroid belt, none of our spacecraft has yet had to deal with it. But even when they do it shouldn't cause too much trouble.

Why not? Won't they have to dodge in and out of the asteroids to avoid getting smashed?
Not really. They'll probably fly straight through. Although there are lots of them, the belt is still so wide that the average distance between two neighbouring asteroids is about a million miles. This is because the gravitational pull of Mars and Jupiter keep them spread out. So while future astronaut pilots may have to steer occasionally, no last-minute dodging manoeuvres will be needed.

Pah. Bor-ing. So where did all these big rocks come from?

Essentially, they're leftovers, bits of the early solar system that didn't become part of the Sun or planets. Jupiter's massive gravitational pull probably prevented the ones in the asteroid belt from clumping into a dwarf planet, whilst the rocky fragments in the Kuiper belt are probably too spread out to attract each other at all. So most float alone in Space, with some occasionally being pulled inwards to become Near-Earth Objects (NEOs) and comets.

Comets come from the Kuiper belt too?

Actually, we think that most of them originate from far further out – from an immense shell of rocky, icy objects that exists far outside our solar system, known as the **Oort cloud**. Most comets spend most of their time way out beyond the solar system, only being pulled inwards to lap the Sun once every million years or so. A few, however, are captured by the gravity of Jupiter or other planets as they get closer to the Sun, and enter new, smaller orbits within the boundaries of the Kuiper belt. It's these comets that we're typically more familiar with, since they come back around often enough for us to notice. **Comet Halley**, for example, passes Earth once every 75–6 years, and it's due back in 2061.

Blimey. That's a bit of a wait.

That's nothing. Comet Hale-Bopp – last spotted in April 1997, and probably the most spectacular-looking comet in recent history – is on its way back towards the Oort cloud, and won't be back again until AD **4531**. So, if you didn't spot that one the first time, I'm afraid you've definitely missed it!

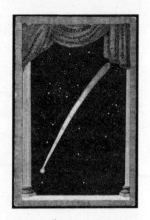

FAMOUS COMETS

Name	Orbital period	Last seen	Due back
Halley's Comet, or Comet Halley	75–6 years	1986	AD 2061
Swift-Tuttle	134 years	1992	AD 2126
Hale-Bopp	2,533 years	1997	AD 4531
Hyakutake	14,000 years	1996	AD 15996

What's the difference between an asteroid and a comet, anyway?

Not much – except that comets grow tails as they near the Sun, and generally contain a lot more ice. In fact, these two things are linked.

Comets are basically big, dirty snowballs that orbit the Sun. Close up, as NASA's **Deep Impact** probe discovered when it smashed into comet **Tempel 1** back in July 2005, they look much like asteroids. The nucleus (or centre) of a comet is made of ice and dust surrounded by a rocky crust. When the comet lies far from the Sun, this is pretty much all there is to see. But, as it approaches and heats up, the nucleus becomes surrounded by a coma (or body), formed as radiation from the Sun blasts a cloud of ice and dust away from the nucleus. This cloud trails behind the comet as it orbits, creating one of its two tails.

Comets have two tails?
Yep. One curving **dust tail**, and a second, straighter **ion tail**, which is formed as charged particles (or ions) are swept away from the comet by the solar wind. The effect of this is that the comet looks as if it's whizzing through Space, with its two tails flailing out behind. But, as a matter of fact, the tail doesn't always trail behind the comet at all. It may look that way as the comet moves towards the Sun. But once it has lapped it and is on its way back to the outer solar system, the tail actually trails *in front* of the comet, *leading* its motion.

If you think about what's happening, this makes sense. The radiation and solar wind that form the tails only travel in one direction. So while the comet approaches the Sun 'into the wind', it travels away with the 'wind' behind it. So as it leaves the solar system, a comet has its tail 'blown' ahead of it – a bit

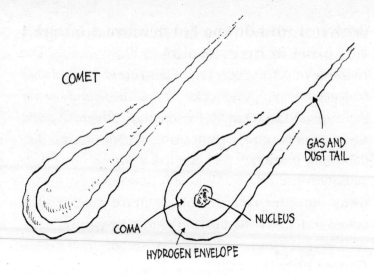

COMET

GAS AND
DUST TAIL

NUCLEUS

COMA

HYDROGEN ENVELOPE

like when you ride a bike with the wind behind you,
and your hair flops forward over your eyes!

Unless you wear a cap or something.
Sorry?

If you wore a cap, that wouldn't happen.
Err . . . right . . .

But I guess comets don't wear caps, do they?
No. No, they don't.

Pity. That'd be mad cool.

Which would do the Earth more damage – a comet or an asteroid?

That one could go either way. Comets and asteroids are basically just big flying rocks, so it all depends how big they are, and how fast they're moving. Either one could wipe out all life on the planet, if it was big enough. But, thankfully, that doesn't happen too often.

Okay – give it to me straight. Will a comet or asteroid destroy the Earth one day, or what?

Well, even the largest comet or asteroid couldn't *destroy the planet*. The planet Earth is just too big. But a big enough impact could destroy most or all of the *life* on Earth, yes. And impacts like this aren't unheard of, either. As recently as 1994, Comet Shoemaker-Levy smashed into Jupiter after breaking into several pieces, leaving scars on it for months afterwards. If just one of those larger fragments had struck the Earth, rather than Jupiter, it would have killed everything on the planet except maybe bacteria*.

Great. What about asteroids?

Large asteroids have probably struck the Earth and caused mass extinctions at least twice in the Earth's history, but we haven't had a biggie for a while. The last large object to strike the Earth (technically,

---

* Plus, the material blown into Space by the impact would have given us a second moon. Which would've been nice, if only there were people left alive to enjoy it!

it exploded above the ground, but you get what I mean) was the Tunguska meteoroid, which exploded over Siberia in 1908 with the force of a nuclear bomb. Thankfully, it didn't destroy anything beyond a few thousands trees in the forests beneath. But a similar-sized asteroid 'buzzed' the Earth in March 2009, missing us by just 44,000 miles (70,000 km) – a mere whisker in Space terms. That one's due back in March 2067, and looks on course to miss again. But there are plenty of other NEOs lurking out there, and it's probably just a matter of time before a big un whacks us.

Yagghhh! That's not very good, is it? So what can we do about it?

Astronomers and Space agencies worldwide are already working to locate and track as many NEOs as they can, in an effort to figure out which ones may pose a threat, and give us as much advance warning as possible before it happens. Much of this is part of the NASA Spaceguard project, which was kicked off in 1992 with a goal of mapping at least 90 per cent of the NEOs up there within ten years.

Beyond that, we're also trying to figure out how we'd deal with it if we found out a comet or asteroid was going to hit us soon. We probably couldn't blow a big one up (at least not without creating a bunch of equally dangerous fragments), so other ideas include trying to blast it off course while it's still some way off.

Or even attaching a 'Space Sail' that will cause it to be blown off course by the solar wind!

The good news is there are no signs of any dangerous asteroids or comets just yet, and it may be thousands of years before there's another impact big enough to cause massive, planet-wide extinctions.

But what happens if we do find one that big? What then?
Well, if we spot it in time, and provided we have the technology, one final option could be to hop the planet and live in Space, or colonize another planet or moon.

And that's what we'll be looking at in the next chapter. This brings us to the end of our tour of the solar system. Now we leave the asteroid belts and comet clouds behind, and we're on our way home.

That's good. I'm hungry, and I could use a bath.
You're telling me.

What?
Nothing.

Hmmmm.
Don't get too comfortable, anyway, as next we'll be back out into the great beyond – to look at travelling and living in Space, and to explore the far reaches and distant future of the Universe.

Sounds good.

It will be. Now go and change your socks and under-pants. *Please.*

Build a solar system!

Group the twenty items into the five correct
categories. Draw lines between category and item.

Categories	Items
	Ceres
Terrestrial planet	Makemake
	Mars
	Halley's
	Titan
Jovian planet	Jupiter
	Uranus
	Shoemaker-Levy
	2009 DD45
Moons	Mercury
	Eris
	Charon
	Neptune
Dwarf planet	Saturn
	Earth
	Pluto
	Venus
Asteroid/comet	Europa
	Hale-Bopp
	Ganymede

(answers on page 253)

6.
The Great Beyond

How long before we travel to other planets and galaxies?

Difficult to say exactly, but it's likely to be at least another twenty or thirty years before we make it to Mars. Beyond that, other planets and galaxies will have to wait until we have more money or better technology. Probably both.

I thought we already had the technology for Space travel. We've been whizzing about in Space for years, haven't we?

In a way, yes. Russian cosmonaut Yuri Gagarin blasted into orbit on 12 April 1961, becoming the first human being in Space. Since then, there have been hundreds of manned Space flights and missions – most undertaken by the USA and former Soviet Union.

Just under a decade after we blasted the first Earthling into orbit, we landed two men on the Moon. Another decade later, in 1981, NASA launched the first Space shuttle on its first orbital mission – the world's first fully reusable spacecraft, designed to help make space exploration cheaper, easier and more routine.

To people growing up in the 1970s and 80s, it seemed like Space travel had literally taken off, and it wouldn't be long before we would all be flying to the Moon for a game of zero-gravity football, or skiing down the snow-capped mountains of Mars. The excitement spilled on to television and the big screen, as the original *Star Trek* series and *Star Wars* films became huge hits with viewers across the globe. How long could it be, people thought, before we were journeying to other galaxies, meeting alien tribes and civilizations, just like in the movies? Another ten, twenty years, maybe?

Yeah – how long *will* it be? I mean, it's *been* more than twenty years, right?
Right. Thirty, in fact, since the launch of the Space shuttle. And fifty years since the first manned Space flight.

So what's the hold-up? Come on, NASA – get a move on! I've got aliens to meet, people to see . . .
Haven't we all. But we're not ready to go just yet, I'm afraid. There's still quite a bit of work to do, and a bunch of problems to solve, before we can hop the planet to Mars and beyond.

But didn't we go to the Moon already? I know Mars is a bit further away, but it can't be *that* much harder to get there, can it?
Well, we did do a great job getting to the Moon, which was already a very long way to go. But Mars is *much* further off. Try the exercise below, and you'll get some idea of just *how much* further.

See for yourself – make a scale model of the Earth-Moon-Mars system!

1) Grab a packet of balloons, a golf ball and two friends.
2) Grab a large, blue balloon, and inflate it until it's roughly 20 cm (8 inches) wide. This is your **Earth**.
3) Now grab the golf ball. This is your **Moon**, and at roughly 5 cm (2 inches) across, it should be more or less to scale against your blue balloon Earth.
4) Hold your Earth aloft, give the Moon to a friend and tell him to walk 6 m (20 feet) away, and hold it up. This, to scale, is how far the Apollo astronauts had to go to land on the Moon.
5) Now let's try adding **Mars**. Grab a red balloon.
6) To make it the right size (to the same scale as the Earth and Moon), inflate it to 11 cm (4 inches).
7) Give it to your other friend, and tell him to keep walking until he's at the right distance from the Earth. How far is that, you ask? Well, to keep your Earth-Moon-Mars system to scale, your friend will have to walk three-quarters of a mile (1.2 km) away with his red balloon. Tell him so.
8) Now ignore the groans, dodge the Moon when your friend throws it at you and try not to be too upset when the other friend pops your Earth and Mars.

That exercise should've given you a more realistic idea of just how far a spacecraft would have to go to reach Mars – let alone more distant planets, solar systems and galaxies. It might also help explain why, in all those hundreds of missions, only *nine* made it to lunar orbit, and why none have yet gone any further than that.

Really?

Yep. Despite over fifity years of manned Space travel, humankind has yet to make it more than about 250,000 miles (400,000 km) away from the Earth. In fact, the vast majority of manned Space missions travel less than 1,000 miles (1,600 km) away – barely more than the length of Great Britain. And we haven't been back to the Moon since 1972.

Since the 1970s? Did the astronauts all wear flared trousers and flowery suits, then?

On the Moon? No.

Oh.

But at home . . . possibly.

Why haven't we landed on Mars yet?

In a way, we already have. We've landed several robots and probes on Mars, and mapped large chunks of its surface. But if you mean 'why only robots, and not people', then it's because manned Space missions are much more difficult and expensive than unmanned probes. This also explains why we haven't been back to the Moon, either.

So why haven't there been more?
You mean more manned missions to the Moon and Mars?

That's a lot of 'M's. But yes – that. I mean, I get that it's a long way and everything, but we've put robot *cars* on Mars, right? And sent probes right out past Saturn. So what's the problem with sending people?
The problem is that while Space probes are (relatively) cheap and easy to launch, manned Space missions are neither. Putting people on a spacecraft makes it much, much heavier, and therefore far more difficult to launch and manoeuvre.

But astronauts don't weigh that much, do they?
Not by themselves. But having real, live people on a spacecraft means you also have to pack it with everything they need to survive.

Like food and water? Come on – how much can they really eat?

You'd be surprised. Remember, a mission to Mars and back would take at least **two and a half years** at the speeds currently achievable by today's rockets and shuttles. That's a lot of cornflakes and chocolate bars! And, aside from food and water supplies, manned spacecraft also need weighty life-support systems to keep the astronauts alive.

These systems include heavy tanks filled with oxygen and nitrogen gas (to provide fresh air), mechanical pumps and filters (to 'scrub' the air of the toxic carbon dioxide that builds up as the astronauts breathe), plus heaters, coolers, sensors, gauges and other machines used to control the temperature and pressure inside the spacecraft. Add that lot up, and you've got several tonnes of extra weight to deal with, and several billion dollars more spent on equipment and fuel.

Hang on – why would you need more fuel?

Well, for starters, it takes a lot more fuel to get a heavier spacecraft off the ground and into Space (more on that in a minute). Plus, with live astronauts instead of robots, you have to worry about *getting the craft back again*, doubling the length of any trip. Robots and probes can simply be abandoned when the mission's over (or when the batteries run out!). But astronauts have to come home. And that means more fuel for the return journey, plus extra equipment (like heat shields, parachutes and floats or wheels) for re-entry and landing.

These are the main reasons why very few manned Space missions ever go beyond a low Earth orbit – exactly where we started, back in 1961. And it's also why it has been almost forty years since we were last on the Moon. Here's a brief history for you:

HUMANS IN SPACE – FAMOUS DATES AND HIGHLIGHTS

12 April 1961

Russian Cosmonaut Yuri Gagarin becomes the first man in Space, aboard the rocket *Vostok 1*. His capsule circled the Earth once before landing in the Sarator region of Russia.

February 1962

John Glenn, Jr becomes the first American astronaut in orbit, three years into NASA's Project Mercury programme. His *Friendship 7* capsule was carried into Space by the Mercury Atlas 6 rocket.

March 1965	Russian cosmonaut Alexey Leonov leaves the *Vokshod 2* capsule to complete the world's first spacewalk. A few months later, in preparation for later *Apollo* moon-landing missions, US astronauts Frank Borman and James Lovell, Jr spend over 300 hours in Space (and orbit the Earth over 200 times) learning to manoeuvre and dock their *Gemini VII* craft. One year later, astronaut Neil Armstrong nearly dies aboard *Gemini VIII*.
May 1969	Astronauts Thomas Stafford, John Young and Eugene Cernan orbit the Moon aboard *Apollo 10*. The spacecraft's lunar module drops to within 9 miles (14 km) of the Moon's surface for a successful test, but doesn't land.
20 July 1969	Neil Armstrong and Edwin 'Buzz' Aldrin successfully land the *Apollo 11* lunar module on the surface of the Moon (while less-famous astronaut Michael Collins

good-naturedly stays in the orbiter module to make sure they get back okay). In a television broadcast to the whole world, Armstrong utters the immortal words: 'That's one small step for man . . . one giant leap for mankind.' Then he plants an American flag, picks up about 22 kg of moon rock and returns home.

April 1970	The ill-fated *Apollo 13* mission almost ends in disaster as an oxygen canister explodes, causing all the spacecraft's systems to fail, and NASA struggles to bring the crew home alive. The three astronauts, James Lovell, Jr; Fred Haise, Jr; and John Sweigert, very nearly suffocate, and barely make it back to Earth after using their landing module as a lifeboat.
11 December 1972	Harrison Schmitt and (hooray!) Eugene Cernan become the last men to walk on the Moon, aboard *Apollo 17*. No further landings have since been attempted by the US or Russia (whose accompanying *Soyuz* programme failed to land even one cosmonaut on its surface).

Since the last moon landing, there have been hundreds more manned Space missions, including over 130 carried out aboard NASA's fleet of reusable Space shuttles. And astronauts from all over the world – including Canada, Europe, Israel, China and Japan – have now made the journey into orbit.

But while more and more countries have joined in Space exploration, and the USA has begun making long-term plans to land a team of astronauts on Mars, many challenges still remain.

And most of them, it seems, come from the problems of attempting long-distance Space travel in heavy craft with feeble rocket power and the huge amount of money it would cost.

Space flight: actually, it *IS* rocket science

With our current rocket technology, a manned flight to Mars would be like rowing a beached aircraft carrier across the Atlantic. If you could get the thing off the beach, into the water and pointed in the right direction, you might just make it. But it'd take a very long time, and few would want to try.

Wait a minute – how can you say rockets are like rowing boats? Rockets are *well* powerful, aren't they? They're way faster than jet aeroplanes, and those are pretty speedy, right?

Right. The fastest jets can do up to 2,200 mph (3,500 kph), whereas a Space shuttle in orbit can top 18,000 mph (28,000 kph). No contest.

There you go, then.

But even at 18,000 mph, it would still take around eighteen months to travel the 50 million miles (80 million km) to Mars*. And, just like our beached aircraft carrier, the main problem isn't going the distance – it's launching the thing in the first place. Spacecraft are much, much heavier than aeroplanes,

---

* This is the average distance between Mars and the Earth. But depending on where they are in their orbits, they could be anywhere from 23 million miles (38 million km) to 150 million miles (250 million km) apart. In any case – it's a *long* way, and would take a *long* time, even at shuttle speed.

and far harder to get off the ground.

Why don't they just build them smaller and lighter, then, like jet planes?

Not a bad idea. But unfortunately we can't. Because spacecraft have to deal with different forces and environments to aeroplanes, they need a different type of engine. A powerful one, which can reach much higher speeds than a jet engine, but also uses far more fuel to do so.

A rocket engine?

Exactly. Even if it could fly in Space (which it can't, as jet engines need an air supply to work, and there's none of that in Space), a jet aeroplane could never reach the speeds needed to escape the Earth's gravitational pull and whizz off into Space – otherwise known as **escape velocity**.

But why does it have to go so fast? Couldn't we just point the jet straight up, like a rocket, and keep going?

Sadly, no. It's a bit like throwing a tennis ball straight up into the air – it would keep going up for a while, but eventually gravity would pull it back down. Even if you fired the tennis ball out of a high-speed cannon, and it went thousands of metres up into the air, friction from the air around it would gradually slow it down, and the ball would eventually be pulled back down again before it could make it into Space.

Now the jet might fare a little better than the tennis ball, but the principle is the same. The engines could only accelerate the jet to a maximum of a few thousand miles per hour, and couldn't even maintain that speed for long. In the thin upper atmosphere, the air would become too thin for the engines to work properly, and they would quickly burn through their limited fuel supply. Eventually (and way before the aircraft could leave the atmosphere), the engines would be unable to counter the pull of gravity, and the jet aircraft would fall back to Earth, just like the tennis ball.

Okay, so how are rocket engines any different?

For starters, rocket engines carry their own air supply, so don't need air around them, and can continue functioning in the thin air of the upper atmosphere. They also work a bit differently.

Jet engines draw in air, compress it, mix in some jet fuel and explode it – which not only drives the aircraft forward through the air, but also keeps it aloft, as that moving air rushes past the wings. Rockets, on the other hand, have no need for wings or moving air. A rocket engine has no air intake – only a single opening or **exhaust**. Inside the engine, solid or liquid fuel is mixed with an oxygen supply (oxidise) and exploded, sending a mass of burning, expanding gases out of the exhaust, and pushing the spacecraft

Jet

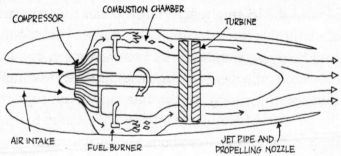

COMPRESSOR
COMBUSTION CHAMBER
TURBINE
AIR INTAKE
FUEL BURNER
JET PIPE AND PROPELLING NOZZLE

Rocket

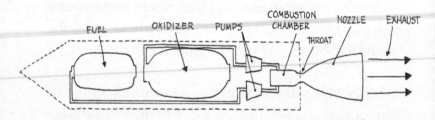

FUEL
OXIDIZER
PUMPS
COMBUSTION CHAMBER
THROAT
NOZZLE
EXHAUST

in the opposite direction. And as long as a fuel supply remains, the burning and exploding keeps going, accelerating the spacecraft to ever greater speeds.

Okay . . .

But here's the thing – in order to reach a speed high enough for the spacecraft to *never* fall back down again (or, rather, get far enough away from the Earth that its gravity can no longer pull it back down), the engines need *lots and lots* of fuel. In fact, around 90 per cent of the weight of a US Space shuttle or Russian rocket is *just the fuel supply*. So in order to get our rocket into Space, we have to pack it with millions of tonnes of heavy fuel. And until we develop some other kind of super-light, super-powerful propulsion system, we *have to* build our spacecraft heavy. But, thankfully, the rocket scientists still have a few tricks up their sleeves . . .

Why do bits drop off rockets on the way up?
To help shed weight and accelerate the orbiter, lander or command module to a very high speed. Without reaching this speed, the spacecraft would never escape the pull of the Earth's gravity, and would fall back down to Earth before it could enter (or leave) orbit.

Hang on . . . what, now? How does breaking apart help it speed up? Isn't a rocket just a big pointy Space missile?
Early rockets were much like missiles, yes. In fact, the earliest rockets *were* missiles – developed by the Chinese for use in battle. Like missiles, they went up in one piece, and came down in much the same shape. But the Vostok rocket used to launch Yuri Gagarin into orbit, and the *Saturn V* rocket used to send the crew of *Apollo 11* to the Moon, were quite different. They were designed in sections which would be jettisoned on the way up.

What? But isn't that a bit dangerous for the astronauts?

Not if it's done properly, and the rocket is *designed* that way.

But why would they *want* to bust their rockets up?

Simple. To lose weight.

We've already learned that rockets are heavy because they need lots of fuel to get off the ground and up to escape velocity. But almost all the fuel a rocket needs is used up during the launch and acceleration into orbit (or beyond). After that, it doesn't need much fuel at all. Since there's no air and no friction in Space to slow the rocket down, it will keep going in the same direction (with the same speed) forever. It'll either orbit round and round the planet, or head off into Space on a straight course – until the pilot gives it a reverse blast with the engines or thrusters to slow it down or bring it out of orbit.

So . . .

So the rocket only needs lots of fuel to get up there – it doesn't need much at all to get back down. With that in mind, the Vostok and Saturn V rocket bodies were designed in breakable stages, which could be dropped off once the engines within had used up all their fuel. The bonus to this approach is that every time the rocket drops a stage, it speeds up – since there's less weight for the remaining engines to lift. So the rocket gets lighter – and faster – the higher up it goes. And that's a great recipe for overcoming gravity and lifting the orbiter or command module into Space.

The Space shuttle does much the same thing. The orbiter (the bit that looks like an aeroplane) forms only a small portion of its weight on the launchpad. The rest is taken up by the immense **external fuel tank** (or **belly tank**) attached to its underside, and the two solid-fuel **booster rockets** attached to the sides. The main engines (fuelled by the belly tank) lift the craft off the ground. A few minutes after lift-off, the fuel in the boosters is used up, and the boosters are dropped, accelerating the now-lighter craft towards orbital velocity. For a minute or so more, the orbiter's main engines continue to burn fuel from the belly tank, until that too is empty. Then guess what happens.

The belly tank drops off?

Exactly. Which speeds up the orbiter even further. Now 90 per cent lighter and going like a bat out of hell, the orbiter easily reaches orbital velocity, and cuts its engines to enter an effortless orbital path around the Earth. To leave orbit and head towards the Moon or another planet, all it would have to do is leave the engines running a while longer, and blast through a little more fuel. In practice, the Space shuttle has never actually done this – since it was designed as a cheap, reusable spacecraft for missions in low-Earth orbits. But the principle is the same for all rockets. Drop weight after launch, and it's easier to reach orbital then escape velocity. And once you've done that it takes relatively little power (and fuel) to steer the craft towards a new course, or drop it out of orbit to bring it back to Earth.

So if it only takes a bit of power to steer it about in Space, why couldn't they just launch a Space shuttle towards Mars or another planet?
Well, they could. But steering it towards Mars wouldn't be the big problem. Landing, on the other hand, probably would. The Space shuttle uses very little fuel to return to Earth, because it basically just slows down and glides home. A quick turn and a blast of the engines slows it enough to bring it out of orbit and falling towards Earth. Then the pilot keeps the nose up and glides through the atmosphere, using the friction from the surrounding air to slow the craft down from over 200,000 to a few hundred miles per hour. Then as the orbiter glides towards the specially built landing strip, it deploys parachutes to bring it down to less than 100 mph – a safe enough speed to land.

But a Space shuttle hurtling towards Mars would have difficulty doing the same thing. It would have to be aimed just right in order to avoid smacking head-on into the planet (or, more likely, burning up in its atmosphere before ever reaching the ground. If the pilot managed to steer and slow it into orbit around

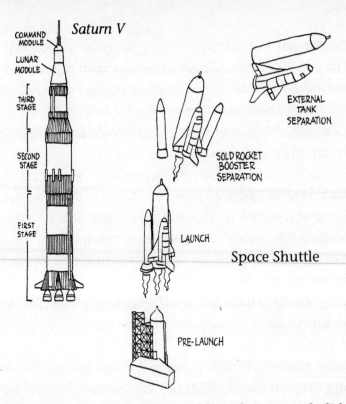

Saturn V

COMMAND
MODULE

LUNAR
MODULE

THIRD
STAGE

SECOND
STAGE

FIRST
STAGE

EXTERNAL
TANK
SEPARATION

SOLD ROCKET
BOOSTER
SEPARATION

LAUNCH

Space Shuttle

PRE-LAUNCH

Mars, there's a chance he could guide it in and glide it into a rough landing (hopefully having dodged all the Martian mountains and canyons) much the same way as it would on Earth.

Brilliant! There you go!
But even if they managed that, there would be no way to get home, as without boosters and more fuel at the 'other end' they'd be unable to lift off. They'd be marooned on Mars. Which is a good name for a science-fiction movie, but a rubbish state of affairs to be in if you're an astronaut.

Oh. I see.
That said, NASA almost certainly wouldn't use a shuttle for a Mars landing anyway. And there have been other designs suggested for rockets and landers that would be able to land people on Mars's surface . . . and hopefully get them back again.

Many of these ideas include plans for spacecraft built and launched *in Space* – from orbiting space stations, or even off-planet Moon bases. And, realistically, Space stations or bases like this will probably have to come before any attempt to land on Mars. That's because – before we send anyone on a three-year return trip – we still need to learn a lot about how to keep astronauts alive in Space for long periods of time. Especially if we're thinking of staying there any longer than a day or two once we arrive. If you're building an off-planet Space base, it'd be far better to test it closer to home first before arriving on Mars and finding it doesn't . . . err . . . work. So for these reasons, Space stations and Moon bases may be the way forward – stepping stones towards a full-on mission to Mars.

Cool! So have they built any yet?
Well, although NASA has started some early plans for a US Moon base, it doesn't look like they'll be able to afford it any time soon. With Space stations, however, we're doing much better . . .

How long before we start building Space stations and Moon bases?

While we haven't managed any Moon bases yet, we have already built and manned not one but ten orbiting Space stations. And several countries are planning Moon bases for the not-too-distant future.

Really? Ten real-life, working Space stations?
Yep. Believe it. NASA built and launched an orbiting science laboratory called SkyLab in 1973. Russia built and manned another seven of them as part of its Salyut Space station testing programme which ran from 1973 to 1991.

Wicked! So are they all still up there now, with people living in them?
Sadly, no. Just one is. The Salyut, SkyLab and Mir stations reached the end of their useful working lives, though we learned a lot of essential things from them. All but the International Space Station have been abandoned, then de-orbited. But the ISS is still up there and still growing, with over fourteen countries worldwide contributing equipment and materials for its construction.

So what's it like? Does it have docks for spaceships and bits with zero gravity and stuff?
It does have docking modules for visiting shuttles and

soyuz and progress modules, yes. And the whole thing is zero gravity*, since we've yet to develop a station with artificial gravity for residents. It's about 73 m (240 feet) long and 108 m (360 feet) wide – about the same as a football pitch. But that includes the width of the solar panels and other external parts of the station. The actual living and working space is limited to a series of wide, tubular modules connected by hatches. It's pretty much equivalent to crawling about inside two cluttered jumbo-jet cabins.

---

* Or, rather, very low gravity, since there's always *some* gravity about in Space. In fact, the pull of gravity on the ISS is about 10 per cent less than at the surface of the Earth, but its constant, free-falling orbit around the Earth makes all the astronauts inside float weightlessly about, anyway. So it feels more or less the same as a zero gravity state.

They have to crawl about the station? They can't just walk or bounce, like on the Moon?

Not really. While the Moon's lower gravitational pull makes astronauts lighter, it still pulls them downwards, toward its centre. The ISS is in free-falling orbit around the Earth, which leaves the people inside drifting and floating in mid-air.

When Space stations were first suggested it was thought that we might be able to simulate on-board gravity by building them like spinning tubes or wheels. That way, the centrifugal force* generated by the spinning station would stick the astronauts to the walls, and they could walk around on them as if they were floors. If you got the spin rate just right, the push back against your feet from the walls would feel almost exactly the same as the push back from the ground that you get as gravity pulls you downwards on Earth. So you could be strolling about your Space station, look up and see a friend walking upside down on the ceiling.

That would be *brilliant*!

Unfortunately, it turns out that building a spinning station like this is trickier than it seems. The craft would have to be very strong to withstand the

---

* This is the force that throws you towards the outside of a spinning object. If – like me – you ever went on a playground roundabout when you were little, and the 'big boys' sped it up until you were flung off it with a painful crash . . . then you've experienced centrifugal forces.

spinning forces, and it would take loads of power (and fuel) to get it up to speed.

So, instead, all the Space stations we've built to date – including the ISS – are of the non-spinning variety. And the preferred way to get about is either to crawl and pull your way along the walls, or to push off a solid wall or object with your hands or feet and glide towards your destination like Superman. Sometimes adding in a quick somersault for extra style points.

Cool! That sounds even better than walking on the ceiling . . .

The latter is far more fun, obviously. But the astronauts and cosmonauts can't get too carried away with it, as they have to be careful not to damage fragile equipment, or themselves, while they gleefully tumble about. It's not all just fun and games up there, you see. They also have work to do.

So what do they do all day?

Experiments, mostly. They test equipment, grow biological cells and give each other physical check-ups to learn about the effects of living in Space. Eventually, NASA and others hope to use Space stations like the ISS as a stopping or launching point for long-distance Space missions. One day, we may be able to assemble spacecraft in Space, using Space stations like orbiting shipyards. This would let us build bigger, heavier craft, as you would only have to launch the pieces up into orbit, rather than the whole ship at once. But for now the ISS is being used to learn more about how machines and living organisms function in Space. Once we've learned enough, we can then progress to bigger, better orbital Space stations, and from there to ground bases on the Moon and other planets.

But why didn't the *Apollo* astronauts just build a base on the Moon while they were up there before, so others could go back and stay?

Firstly, they didn't have long enough. They were only on the Moon for a few hours – long enough to take a few snaps, drive a short distance in the lunar rover, collect a few rock samples and do a few experiments on the surface. Secondly, the *Apollo* spacecraft was only powerful enough to land the crew on the Moon. It had nowhere near enough power (or fuel) to carry all the material needed to build a working Moon base. And, thirdly, no one had designed or tested a working Moon base before. And, in fact, they still haven't.

What? How hard could it be? I mean, it's basically just a big Space tent for camping out on the Moon, right?

Kind of. Except that normal campers don't have to worry about their tent being airtight, pressurized, temperature-controlled, and radiation-shielded. Plus it has to be big enough to house all the food, water and equipment the astronauts will need for months on end. And since the 'Moon campers' can't leave the tent all of their sweat, dead skin cells and – ahem – other bodily wastes will pile up inside unless they can be recycled or disposed of.

Urgh. Gross. Never thought of it like that. Right. Keeping the base freshly supplied and . . . err . . . fresh in general are the two major problems involved with off-planet living.

LIVING IN SPACE

Space stations and spaceships might sound like the coolest homes imaginable, but there's more to life in Space than just floating about and star-spotting through the portholes. Conditions are tough, and it takes a lot of work just to survive and stay healthy.

Exercise is essential, since your muscles begin to waste away in low-gravity environments. Astronauts on the ISS use treadmills and exercise bikes every day to stay strong and fit.

Eating isn't as easy as you might think. To save on weight, Space foods normally come in dehydrated packages, and the choices are pretty limited. And liquids float up out of cups, leaving you to chase blobs of water or lemonade like a gulping goldfish. Unless you drink everything through a straw.

Sleeping can be difficult too when the ship or Space station orbits the Earth so fast that the Sun rises every ninety minutes. Plus you have to be zipped into wall-mounted sleeping bags to stop your arms and legs flailing about in your sleep (or, worse yet, drifting unconscious into the toilet).

Toilets: speaking of which, trips to the loo can be quite an ordeal in Space too. Remember what we just said about liquids in low-gravity? Exactly. If you 'sprinkle while you tinkle' on a Space station, you'll be wiping down more than just the toilet seat. As a result, astronauts have to use chemical toilets that work a bit like vacuum cleaners. You can probably imagine the rest. And what happens if they malfunction . . . ?

That said, several nations are hoping to return to the Moon within the next twenty years, for exploratory missions or to build temporary or permanent bases. The US and India are planning to arrive by 2020, China want their own Moon landing (and a start on their own Moon base) by 2022, and Europe, Russia and Japan are aiming to join the party by 2025.

What about bases on Mars or other planets? Any plans for those?
No solid plans just yet. NASA has planned a new space programme – called Constellation – that could get us there. But at the moment it has been stalled due to a lack of funds from the US government. If it ever does get the money, the programme's three main goals would be:

1) Build the next generation of spacecraft to replace the retired Space shuttle fleet
2) Return to the Moon and establish a 'long-term human presence' there (i.e. build a Moon base)
3) Use the new craft to shuttle explorers to the ISS, the Moon and 'possibly to Mars and beyond'

'Beyond' could eventually include Europa, Titan or other candidates for life within the solar system. But all that would be a very long way off.

Right now, with so little money available to fund new rockets and missions, scientists are still arguing about whether we should continue with the 'stepping stone' approach (from Moon base to Mars base), or just skip the Moon and head straight for Mars. The future of Space exploration is, in a way, wide open. For NASA, it would all depend on the success of its new rocket fleet. If they proved to be rapid and reliable replacements for the Space shuttles, then Moon bases and Mars missions may not be too far behind. But if they turned out to be an expensive flop it would be difficult to find the money for more than a few trips to the ISS and back.

What would the new spaceships be like? Like newer, bigger Space shuttles?

Not really. In fact, they would look more like the *Saturn V* rockets and modules that carried the *Apollo* teams to the Moon all those years ago. After a series of safety problems with the Space shuttles, NASA went back to the drawing board, and is planning to build a fleet of more traditional 'tower' rockets with cone-shaped crew vehicles like the *Apollo* command modules. The *Ares* launch vehicle and *Orion* crew exploration module would carry astronauts to the orbiting ISS and, later, would leave Earth's orbit to swing around the Moon. Once there, the new *Altair* lunar lander would take a new generation of astronauts down to walk in Neil Armstrong's and Gene Cernan's footsteps. Which should still be there even twenty years from now, since there's no wind or rain on the Moon to break them up.

Who knows – maybe one of those astronauts could be you . . .

What's the furthest we've gone across the Universe?

Our astronauts and cosmonauts have yet to make it any further than the Moon, but our unmanned probes and robot explorers have gone much, much further. One has just made it out of the solar system, and another is about to buzz Pluto in its outer reaches.

Is that it? People on the Moon and robots to Pluto? That's not very far, is it?

That depends on how you look at it. Compared to the distance across the Universe, which is billions of light years, then no – it's not very far. But when you understand just how far away it is[*], you realize that putting people on the Moon was no small feat. And NASA's New Horizons probe is currently en route to Pluto – which is over **3.7 billion miles (5.9 billion km)** away – while the Voyager 1 probe has already travelled over 10 billion miles (16 billion km), and made it all the way out of the solar system! It's difficult for us to imagine these kinds of distances, as no two points on the Earth are more than a few thousand miles apart. Multiply that by a *million*, and you're getting somewhere closer to the distances our robot probes have travelled.

---

[*] If you haven't done it already, try the exercise on page 199 to get a better idea of this vast distance.

What about other solar systems and galaxies?
How much further off are they?

Now you're talking light years. Trillions and trillions of miles away. Even the solar system 'next to' ours is over **ten light years (59 trillion miles,** or **94 trillion km) away** – over **16,000** times the distance from here to Pluto. And the closest known *galaxy* to ours, Canis Major, is over **80,000 light years** away. That's roughly **128,000 times the distance from here to Pluto.**

Look at it that way, and you'll see that we haven't done too badly after all. Especially since it was only in 1957 that we launched our first bleeping, ball-like satellite into Space.

That first effort, the Soviet satellite Sputnik 1, made it just a few thousand miles into orbit around the Earth back in 1957. But since then our satellites, probes, explorers and robot rovers have been all over the solar system

The Mariner 4 probe gave us the first close-up snaps of Mars as it whizzed past it in 1964. In the 1970s, the Pioneer Venus probes sent back pictures from the orbit and upper atmosphere of Venus, and the Venera probes landed on it – giving us the first colour pictures of its surface. Meanwhile, the Voyager probes were whizzing around Jupiter, giving us close-ups of its many moons, and the very first surprise glimpse of its rings.

By 1980, Voyager 1 had reached Saturn to take the first detailed (and beautiful) pictures of the ringed giant, and Voyager 2 arrived a year later to take more. After sending back some choice snaps and measurements, it then sped onwards to explore Uranus in 1986, and reached Neptune in 1989.

The 1990s saw the Mars Global Surveyor arrive to begin its mission of mapping the surface of Mars, and the Mars Pathfinder-Sojourner robot rover delighted the world by successfully landing, racing about and sending back pictures from the surface. Then in 2003, NASA engineers got to race not one but two Mars exploration rovers – named Spirit and Opportunity – across different regions of the planet, making every radio-controlled-car fan in the world go green with envy. Oh, and they also discovered a lot about the planet too. Naturally.

And we're not stopping there, either. NASA is planning more rover missions to explore Mars, along with its two moons, **Phobos** and **Diemos**. And this time they're hoping to have the explorer probes return with samples from the Martian surface. In 2016, the Juno probe will be headed off to study Jupiter, and in 2030, there are plans for a Neptune orbiter that will study not just the planet, but also its rings and its mysterious moon, **Triton**. And some of the most exciting missions – to search for signs of life on **Europa**, **Titan**, **Enceladus** and other moons – are still in the works.

What's more, the Pioneer and Voyager probes have all passed the orbit of Pluto and are still going strong!

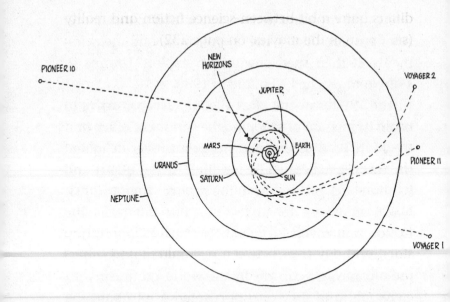

Voyager 1 currently holds the record for the most distant man-made Space probe. It's now over 10 billion miles (16 billion km) from the Sun. So that's the furthest we've gone yet.

Yeah, yeah – that's all pretty impressive, I s'pose. But in the movies spaceships fly between planets and galaxies all the time. How are we supposed to meet any aliens if we can't even get out of the solar system?

Well, in the movies, most of the spaceships seem to be able to travel faster than light, covering the light years between planets in minutes or hours, rather than centuries. That's all good for Hollywood, but it's just one of many things about Space travel that differs quite a bit between science fiction and reality (see Space in the movies, on page 232).

But why?

Unfortunately, as far as we know, faster-than-light travel is not only difficult, but *impossible* – since it would take more energy than exists in the entire Universe to accelerate a spaceship up to light speed, let alone beyond it. So while we may develop much faster rockets (or new types of space-engine) in the future, it may still take years to reach neighbouring stars, and day trips between our galaxy and others are unlikely to become common.

It's a bit like the development of sea travel. It used to take sailing boats months to cross the Atlantic Ocean, but steam-powered ships reduced that to weeks, and jet aeroplanes have now reduced it to hours. But it's still a long way across the ocean, and it still takes time. There's a limit to how fast we can go. Space is like that too. Only the ocean of Space is much, much bigger.

Boo. That's no fun.

That said – our robot probes don't seem to mind spending years on end floating through Space, and we don't have to worry about getting them home again. So until we learn to supercharge our space-ships a bit, they can continue to scout solar systems (and maybe even other galaxies) for us.

And who knows – maybe our first contact with other life-forms may be through one of our robots. Let's just hope the aliens don't get confused, and think we *all* look like that . . .

SPACE IN THE MOVIES

Sci-fi movies and TV series about Space are great fun, and some of them can teach us a lot about stars, planets, moons, gravity, Space flight and more. But many of them get things wrong – either accidentally, or because the reality would be far less exciting to see on screen. Here are five of the most common Space-related boo-boos.

1) **Light-speed travel.** In movies, spaceships often 'warp' through Space at several times the speed of light, covering distances between stars and galaxies in hours, minutes or even seconds. But according to Einstein's General Theory of Relativity, it's impossible to accelerate any mass (including spaceships and Space crews) to the speed of light, as the closer you get to it, the heavier you become, until it becomes practically impossible to get any faster. Maybe one day we could solve this problem by finding ways to travel through 'wormholes' in Space, or even through other dimensions. But unfortunately we're no closer to that than we are to achieving travel at even one-thousandth the speed of light.

2) Sound. As movie spaceships whizz through Space and across our screens, their engines roar and whoosh like jet fighters buzzing the crowd at an airshow. But since there's no air in Space, there's no way for soundwaves to travel through it, and we wouldn't hear a spaceship's engines even if we were floating in Space and the ship whizzed past just a few inches away.

3) Explosions and fire. In *Star Wars* and *Star Trek*, armed spaceships fly through Space and zap at each other with laser beams and Space torpedoes, and when a ship is destroyed, they burst into flames, plunge smoking into moons and asteroids, or explode immediately with a satisfying BOOM. But fiery explosions require oxygen, and with no oxygen in Space there would be no smoke or flames spewing out of an damaged spacecraft. Instead, a damaged craft would most likely **implode** (or crumple inwards on itself), or vent gas and debris into Space like a metallic lawn sprinkler.

4) Lasers. And while we're at it let's talk about laser beams. Lasers are beams of concentrated, focused light. So we can only see the straight path they take through the air if there's something between the laser and the target for the beam to bounce off. Think of a laser pointer – unless the room is full of smoke, you can't see the beam pointing to the wall, only the spot of light as it hits the solid target and bounces back. In Space, there's nothing for a laser to bounce off. So the beams of laser weapons would be invisible too. You'd just see a bright spot on the target, then a crumpling, fizzing spaceship, as detailed above.

5) Gravity. In most sci-fi movies and series, people sit, stand and stroll about as if they're on board ocean-going cruise liners, rather than spacecraft hurtling between stars and planets. In most cases, the crew would be experiencing very different forces and gravitational fields than they would on Earth, yet they rarely – if ever – float out of their seats or crawl along walls and ceilings. Some explain this away by hinting that the spaceship has an on-board 'gravity generator'. But even if it did somehow generate its own (quite large) gravitational field, you'd expect the 'gravity waves' to extend outwards in a sphere from some point in the ship. Why, then, would it just follow the outline of the ship, leaving anyone who spacewalks outside the craft floating weightless in zero-gravity Space?

Hmmmm. Maybe future spaceships are more advanced than we could imagine. Or maybe the budget for most sci-fi movies doesn't stretch to filming in Space or recreating low-gravity conditions . . .

Will we ever reach the end of the Universe?

That depends on what you mean. If you mean 'Will we ever travel to the very edge of the Universe?', the answer is probably no. It's too far off, it's still moving away from us, and there may be no real 'edge' for us to reach, anyway. If you mean 'Will the Universe ever come to an end?', then yes – it probably will. Although we can't say for sure how or when . . .

How far is it to the edge of the Universe, anyway?
To be honest, we don't really know. The part of it we can see (or rather detect, using radiation-sensing instruments) makes the Universe **billions of light years** across. But that almost certainly isn't where the Universe ends – it's just that we can't 'see' any further than that. It's a bit like staring across the sea to the horizon – just because you can't see beyond it, that doesn't mean there's nothing there. Unless, of course, you believe that there's an edge to the world, over which the oceans cascade like a waterfall.

Don't be stupid. Everybody knows the world is round.
There you go, then.

But when you go sailing over the horizon, you

just keep going, because you're going around the world, right?

Right.

So how's that the same as the Universe? I mean, the Universe isn't round, is it?

Not in the same sense as the Earth, no. But some cosmologists (physicists who study the structure and origins of the Universe) think that the Universe could be 'round' in *four dimensions*, rather than three, wrapping around on itself instead of having a defined boundary or edge. If that were true, then – just like on Earth – you'd never get beyond the horizon or 'edge' of the Universe. If you managed to get there at all, you'd just keep on going. And, eventually, your spaceship would go right around the Universe and end up back where you started. Instead of sailing around the world, you'd have taken your ship right around the Universe.

Crazy. It that really possible?

Theoretically, yes. But in practice, probably not. For starters, you'd need a spaceship which could travel at the speed of light*. And even with one of those the journey would take a minimum of 156 billion years. If you survived that long, you'd be roughly twenty-six times older than the planet Earth. Good luck with that.

---

* Which we're fairly sure is impossible – see page 231 for details.

What if the Universe did have an edge, and you had a light-speed spaceship? Then it'd only take half the time, right?

Right. But that's still 78 billion years – still well beyond the age of most planets, let alone people. Plus there's one more slight complication . . .

What's that?

The Universe is still expanding. Most stars and galaxies are moving away from each other as the fabric of the Universe continues to inflate in the aftermath of the Big Bang. So by the time we arrive at the 'edge', it would have expanded outwards, beyond our reach. What's more, because most distant galaxies are whizzing away from us at faster than the speed of light, we'd have trouble catching up with them at all, let alone overtaking them to reach the edge of the expanding Universe.

Yeah, but they can't keep going forever, can they? I mean, they have to slow down sooner or later. Then maybe we could catch up, or overtake. Right?

Well, we used to think maybe that could be the case. We know the Universe has been expanding ever since the Big Bang, but many cosmologists figured that it would eventually run out of energy, slowing, stopping and finally reversing its expansion. Then the Universe would begin contracting towards a **Big**

Crunch, where all the stars, planets and galaxies get closer and closer together until their total mass ends up all crunched up in a ball of infinite density and energy. Hence, the Universe will have gone full circle. If that were so, then at some point – yes – the galaxies would stop fleeing, and an interstellar spaceship could theoretically hop galaxies and reach the edge of the Universe.

But as far as we can tell the expansion of the Universe isn't actually slowing down at all – it's speeding up. Cosmologists aren't sure about why this is happening, but many believe that there is a mysterious phenomenon, termed **Dark Energy**, which is pulling the Universe apart*. If this continues, the Universe will end in one of two ways:

1) It'll keep expanding forever, with stars freezing and winking out as they become too far apart to warm each other and spawn new protostars. We call this the **Big Freeze**.
2) The rate of expansion will become so great that it will literally rip the Universe to pieces, shredding stars, planets, moons and eventually the very atoms they're made of. We call this the **Big Rip**.

---

* There's also a type of invisible matter – called **Dark Matter** – that holds the Universe together with the strength of its gravity. It's like a giant game of tug-of-war between Dark Energy and the gravitational pull of Dark Matter. At any rate, if these things both exist, then it seems that the Dark Energy is winning, as we're still being pulled apart.

So how will the Universe end?

At the moment, it looks like the Big Freeze, but who knows. Other theories say that our Universe is just one of many, and that black holes are giving birth to new 'baby' or 'bubble' universes all the time. Maybe our universe will freeze or fade to black only to be replaced by another one bubbling up from inside it. Maybe there have been many Big Bangs, like water ripples spreading beneath a dripping tap, and our universe is just one more ripple in the fabric of another, larger universe or dimension we can't see.

Whoaaaa. This is doing my head in . . .

Don't worry too much. Whatever the case, it'll be at least another 14 billion years before we have to deal with the Universe coming to an end. So our ancestors should have plenty of time to figure it out.

Have we found any aliens yet?

Contrary to what you may have seen on TV or the internet . . . no, not yet. But we now have a much better idea of what we're looking for, and there are people scouring our galaxy for them as we speak. What's more, thanks to a host of recent discoveries, the odds of finding alien life now look better than ever.

So all those stories about UFO crashes and aliens kidnapping people are . . .

. . . a load of rubbish, yes. Although UFOlogists (as they call themselves) worldwide report sightings of strange lights and aliens visiting their homes almost every week, not one has yet been backed up with any solid evidence. Most of the lights turn out to be normal aircraft, or natural phenomena like lightning and lenticular clouds (which, when lit from a certain angle, look just like flying saucers). Other UFO 'sightings' are faked – often very poorly – using torches by night, and shiny frisbees by day. And a good number of them are simply daft mistakes. Like the lady who telephoned a Welsh police station in 2008 to report a 'bright, circular object hanging in the sky'. It turned out to be the Moon.

But what about alien kidnappings and crop circles and cow mutilations and stuff?

There's no evidence that they're linked to aliens,

either. Alien 'abductees' most often dream or hallucinate their kidnapping ordeals, and only 'recall' details much later on. Some may genuinely believe they were kidnapped, being confused by brain conditions such as temporal lobe epilepsy and sleep paralysis. Others just make it up to get in the papers or on the telly. As for crop circles and cow mutilations, the former are a proven hoax carried out by clever pranksters, while the latter are usually the work of wolves or other wild animals.

Pah. No aliens ever, then?

Well, no aliens *yet*, but that doesn't mean there *never will be*. Many astrobiologists (scientists who combine the study of astronomy and biology to search for extraterrestrial life) believe that alien life may be quite common in the Universe. Some think there may even be alien life lurking somewhere in our solar system . . .

Really? Where?

Well, as we've already seen, Mars and Venus are both out. Been there, done that and came up empty. For a while, scientists were pinning all their hopes on these two planets, since it seemed that it would be impossible for life to survive anywhere else. But now we're not so certain.

Why's that?

Because a few quite recent discoveries have changed

the way we think about life on other worlds, opening up a boatload of new possibilities.

We used to think Mars and Venus were our only hopes for ET life, because these were the only two planets it was possible for life (as we know it) to survive. All the other planets, we thought, would either be too close to the Sun (and therefore too hot), or too far from the Sun (and therefore too cold). Plus every form of life that we know of depends upon liquid water – and Venus and Mars are the only two planets where it might not have long since boiled off or frozen solid.

But when the first robot lander touched down to explore the surface of Venus, it found no water and no life. Just a hellish world too hot, dry and turbulent for any living things to survive. Mars fared little better. Despite all the hopeful scanning and roving with robot cars, no liquid water has been found there, either, nor any sign of Martian life. When these only two candidate planets came up empty, many scientists gave up hope, and started wondering whether Earth might be a rare planet – a uniquely warm and wet haven for life in an otherwise barren solar system. Maybe even the only site for life in the entire galaxy.

But aren't there billions of planets in the galaxy? Wouldn't at least one or two of them be warm and wet like the Earth?

You'd expect so, yes. And we've been trying to find these Earth-like planets in other solar systems for a while now.

Great! So what's the plan – find a decent planet, then buzz over there for a closer look?
Not quite. With our current spacecraft, we're not yet capable of leaving the solar system and reaching other stars. And even unmanned probes could take thousands of years to arrive. But we can send signals and listen for responses. If there's an alien civilization somewhere on Tau Ceti, we might be able to 'ping' them and have them come to us. Or initiate a chat, at the very least.

Cool! But how will we pick up the signals if we don't have alien radios?
Well, we've actually been listening for extraterrestrial radio signals for quite some time, as part of the Search for Extra-Terrestrial Intelligence (SETI) project. To do this, astronomers use huge radio-telescopes, with dishes over 100 m across. But it's not an easy job. The telescope can only focus on a tiny sliver of Space at a time. And not knowing where the aliens might be, the astronomer basically has to pick one target star from among millions, and hope for the best. Hardly surprising, then, that we haven't tuned in to any ET radio just yet.

But once they know where to look, they can aim it there, right?

Right. If they find good candidate planets, these will make much more specific targets for the SETI project, and give us a far greater chance of making contact with an alien race.

But we also have to face the possibility that while life-forms might be common in the Universe (maybe even in our galaxy), advanced alien civilizations with languages, radios and spaceships may not. With that in mind, we're also focusing our alien-life search a little closer to home. As in, within our own solar system.

But I thought you said our solar system was out, cos all the planets except ours were rubbish for life?

Maybe so. But, then again, maybe not. While the other planets in the solar system look like a dry, dead loss, there are still a few possible sites where there may still be liquid water, together with the molecules required to make living cells and structures. NASA probes passing Saturn's moon Encedalus have recently spotted geysers spewing water vapour from beneath its frozen surface, hinting that it may be warmer and wetter under there than previously thought. Jupiter's moon Europa may have an entire ocean of liquid water beneath its solid surface, and even Neptune's moon, Triton, may have flowing water beneath its surface.

Of course, if there is life beneath the seas of these snowball moons, it may not look much like the plants or animals we have here on Earth.

So what would it look like? Like a plant? Or a fish or something?
Without direct heat or light from the Sun, life on these alien waterworlds would be unable to make energy through photosynthesis (as our plants and algae do), and without plants at the bottom of the food chain, it's hard to imagine how larger animals like fish could evolve. If there's life there at all, it'll most probably be in the form of single-celled bacteria or protists (which are single-celled animals that swim or drift about to feed off other life-forms).

Not very exciting, then.
But it's possible that these ET life-forms have evolved in ways we haven't yet seen, to survive in environments we thought could not support life. Even on Earth, a recent exploration of the world's deepest ocean trench – the Marianas Trench – has revealed a whole host of new species that we never could have imagined would survive down there without light or heat from the Sun.

There are giant tube worms which bask and feed in the warm, mineral-rich flows from hydrothermal vents – volcanically heated jets of water that stream from holes in the sea bed. There are giant isopods,

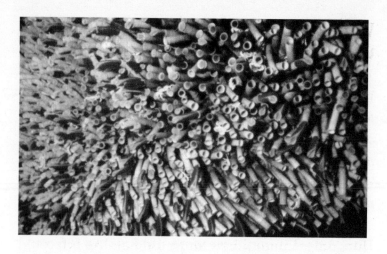

which look like huge, white woodlice measuring up to 30 cm (12 inches) across. And there are giant sea spiders that reach sizes of 76 cm (30 inches) or more. If life can get that weird here on Earth, just imagine how strange the life on Europa or Triton may be. Who knows what we might find.

Giant sea spiders? Yeeuch! Maybe I don't want to meet an alien after all . . .

What would be the best planet for us to live on?

While most of our own solar system remains inhospitable to human life, many other systems in our galaxy could offer more inviting places to stay. In fact, there may be more habitable planets than we ever before imagined. But when all's said and done, the choice for 'best planet' is pretty obvious.

Hang on – I thought we were still looking for other systems and planets like ours?

We are. And we've yet to find another system (or planet) *exactly* like our own. But even if we found it we might not recognize it right away. For starters, it's difficult to make out the details of extrasolar planets, since they're so far away and so small and dim compared to their parent stars. For this reason, most of the extrasolar planets we've spotted so far have been Jupiter-sized gas giants that have no hope of supporting life.

That said, even just within our own galaxy, there are over **100 billion** stars similar in size and temperature to our own Sun, and each one of those could be supporting a solar system with at least one Earth-like planet. That would give us at least 100 billion habitable worlds in our galaxy alone.

Is that why you said 'there may be more than we ever imagined'?

247

It gets better. Those are just the ones in systems like ours – centred on yellow dwarf stars similar to our Sun. But many astronomers now believe that smaller, cooler red dwarf stars may be able to support Earth-like planets too. They may even provide more stable solar systems, since they take longer to burn out, giving extra time for life to evolve on any suitable planets around it.

Excellent!

What's more, some scientists think that many of the systems we've already ruled out – those with the giant, Jupiter-sized gas planets – may be hiding Earth-like planets too. According to one theory, solar systems with massive gas giant planets very close to the central star can arrange themselves in different ways, with the 'Hot Jupiter' pulling rock and ice behind it to form warm, wet, Earth-like planets further from the Sun. About two-fifths of the extrasolar planets discovered so far are 'Hot Jupiters' like these, and every one of them could be hiding a wee earth behind it. This ups the number of potentially inhabitable systems even further.

Brilliant! So when do we leave?
Hang on a minute – what's the rush?

Well, our planet's all messed up, isn't it? There's global warming, and pollution, and wars, and the animals are going extinct . . .

. . . but what makes you think we'd do any better on Earth 2.0?

Well, we'd look after it this time, wouldn't we? Put a stop to all the bad stuff before it got too . . . well . . . bad.

Hmmmm. Perhaps. But here's the thing . . . Firstly, we're still light years (literally) from the *nearest* system that *may* be hiding an Earth-like planet.

Secondly, even if we *had* a way to get there, how would we get **all 6 or 7 billion people** from this planet to that one (assuming we're not leaving people behind)?

And, finally, if we're going to survive long enough to develop the advanced energy and propulsion technologies we need to reach other solar systems and galaxies, we need to take care of our own home first!

You see, for all its problems and difficulties, planet Earth is where we were born to live, and it's still far and away the best planet for us to stay on. Preventing more pollution, wars and environmental destruction on our planet may prove very tricky. And undoing the damage we've already done may prove harder still. But if we're to survive as a species we need to clean our house and take care of what we've got, rather than devour it and move on to the next planet like a swarm of interstellar locusts.

Oh. I didn't think of it like that.

All we need to do is take stock and vow to protect the planet and every one of its many forms of life. The plants and trees. The bats and birds. The dolphins and dingoes. The seals, sharks, snakes and spiders. The lions, tigers, whales and elephants. The ants, the armadillos and ourselves. We need to stop polluting our atmosphere and oceans, stop destroying our forests and other natural habitats. And we need to work together to solve our differences, share our natural resources and stop fighting senseless wars that do little but lose time, money and precious human lives.

That done, a new age of knowledge and wonder awaits us. One day the human race could be one of many known intelligent species in the Universe. We may find ourselves light years from our beginnings as primitive animals staring up at the night sky. Not just looking at the stars, but journeying between them to meet entire alien civilizations.

Aliens who, right now, are gazing across billions of miles of Space at the tiny dot of our bright spiral galaxy . . . from their own world far, far away . . . wondering if we're here, and if they'll ever get to meet us.

Answers

Astronomer word search solution from page 43

```
K U S K F Z J H Y C A B N D F V N J K A
X R F C C X C A E G X E T E V G Z E Y H
O R K O T H H P U L U U C S W M B N Q V
L H K Z I D D E O J I B G O O T K H O X
D V K B C I R T N E C O E G O E O N G A
A M D A N T P U S V C Q C H D L L N X A
R S U C I N R E P O C D L E R T P K N S
U F R I E R X D A Y H W F K N O T V R P
U L X O T B J B W M U H V E S T Q W S W
N T W C S W P W J E I X T P N S R I L T
P N H X N I V Y H L O W K L S I V I X Y
Q E Y T I V A R G O X B D E V R I X C O
K M S C E I R B N T I I M R F A I V X D
O D H P K P Z N C P H R N F W S C M B A
B Q J T I F E Z C J U J C P P O M N J O
D L U E O L U X J O H Q H U M Q V T M G
W U U T R N L Z W X E L X Z E Z J V I W
C E J R B F P E U G P H T G Q X S D M I
N X F A I P T A M Q M C B B U E S Q G O
F R V R T B Y J D I X A J D K K C T J I
```

Stars and galaxies word search solution from page 105

```
Y Q S U K J T T N G R H H X W C J J L S
Y C L Y N T A R E D D W A R F K D R Z U
O M M P Z N X G H R S J R E A P J E U P
U V F R N A C O T O V J Q B T X L H X E
N W M O N I N Y R C U F L V C B P J H R
N W Q T S G N U U L D U V X B V J P H N
D Y E O A E P E Q X Q H G U H G O S R O
G S K S I U V T U F B L H H L O D Q W V
L U Q T R L Q E L Y F I K L Y G P J R A
C P X A H B L E N T I C U L A R C N T O
A E F R Y C V I T T U E V P S L N V U
R R H O O I U E F R H L H U S A R Z C R
A M S N L N H R O P O O K C C P K W V U
L A S E W U U Z K H H W R I K P N O K I
U S P C A G H A K F L O T I Z X O K S M
B S I V I X O C F V Y P S R Z N F D E O
E I R E T G A Q D Q I R S Q K O F A Y Z
N V A H Y L V S A L V T Y Q A V N M B C
R E L V B T H X L G Y M T H T J I F B S
A E V X R I O E T L N U Q Q E O E D E A
```

Planetary sudoku solution from page 178

♄	♆	♃	♀	☉	⊕	☿	♅	♂
♅	☿	♀	♃	♂	♆	♄	⊕	☉
♂	☉	⊕	♄	☿	♅	♃	♀	♆
☉	⊕	♄	♂	♅	♀	♆	♃	☿
♆	♀	♅	☿	♄	♃	♂	☉	⊕
☿	♃	♂	♆	⊕	☉	♅	♄	♀
♀	♄	♆	☉	♃	♂	⊕	☿	♅
⊕	♂	☿	♅	♀	♄	☉	♆	♃
♃	♅	☉	⊕	♆	☿	♀	♂	♄

Build a solar system solution from page 196

Categories	Items
Terrestrial planets	Mercury, Venus, Earth, Mars
Jovian planets	Jupiter, Saturn, Uranus, Neptune
Moons	Pluto, Ceres, Eris, Makemake
Dwarf planet	Titan, Ganymede, Europa, Charon
Asteroid/comet	2009 DD45, Halley's, Shoemaker-Levy, Hale-Bopp

SCIENCE SORTED

Evolution, nature and stuff

Glenn Murphy

How did we develop from chemical soup into internet-surfing human beings?

What is a selfish gene?

What are the kingdoms of life?

Evolution and genetics are like a map
for exploring the whole world of living things.
Trace the history of life right back to our
earliest ancestors and you'll be amazed at
what you find. This book tells you everything
you need to know, with none of the boring bits!

Why is SNOT green?

The First Science Museum Question and Answer Book

Glenn Murphy

Why is snot green? Do rabbits fart? What is space made of? Where does all the water go at low tide? Can animals talk? What are scabs for? Will computers ever be cleverer than people?

Discover the answers to these and an awful lot of other brilliant questions frequently asked at the Science Museum in this wonderfully funny and informative book.

How Loud Can You BURP?

and other extremely important questions (and answers) from the Science Museum

Glenn Murphy

How loud can you burp? Could we use animal poo in power stations to make electricity? Why is water wet, and is anything wetter than water? What's the deadliest disease in the world? What are clouds for?

A second volume of questions and answers from the Science Museum by the author of the mega-bestselling WHY IS SNOT GREEN? A wonderfully funny and informative book with loads of fascinating facts and no boring bits!

Stuff that scares your

PANTS off!

**The Science Museum Book of Scary Things
(and ways to avoid them)**

Glenn Murphy

What scares you most? Spiders or sharks?
Ghosts or aliens? Dentists or darkness?

This amazing book takes apart your deepest,
darkest fears. With a bit of biology, a spot of
psychology and oodles of lovely facts and figures,
you'll learn everything there is to know about the
stuff that scares your pants off.

A selected list of titles available from
Macmillan Children's Books

The prices shown below are correct at the time of going to press.
However, Macmillan Publishers reserves the right to show new retail
prices on covers, which may differ from those previously advertised.

All Pan Macmillan titles can be ordered from our website,
www.panmacmillan.com, or from your local bookshop and
are also available by post from:

Bookpost, PO Box 29, Douglas, Isle of Man IM99 1BQ

Credit cards accepted. For details:

Telephone: 01624 677237

Fax: 01624 670923

Email: bookshop@enterprise.net

www.bookpost.co.uk

Free postage and packing in the United Kingdom